I0039578

The Johnia Berry Story

My Jouney for Justice for Johnia

Joan Berry

Pale Woods Publishing

The Johnia Berry Story

My Journey for Justice for Johnia

Joan Berry

Published September 25, 2023

Pale Woods Publishing

Copyright © 2023 Joan Berry

Front Cover: Sweet 15 Designs, LLC

Knoxville, Tennessee

Print ISBN: 979-8-218-25388-2

E-book ISBN: 979-8-218-25389-9

Library of Congress Control Number: 2023915349

All rights reserved. No part of this book may be reproduced, stored in a retrieval system, or transmitted in any form or by any means, electronic, mechanical, photocopying, recording, or otherwise, without written permission from the author. Brief quotations may be used in articles or reviews. For permission requests, write to the publisher at

turnerco6@yahoo.com

This book is a work of non-fiction. Names, characters, businesses, places, events, and incidents are the product of the author's personal knowledge or permission granted by those who contributed pieces to publish their work.

To my dearest Johnia...
Having you for twenty-one years was better than never having you at all.

Foreword

I will never forget the first time I saw Joan Berry.

My cameraman and I arrived at a home in Johnson City, Tennessee, owned by a friend who'd offered to facilitate Joan's first local television interview since her daughter's murder in December 2004. Turns out, my friend knew and loved Johnia and Joan for many years. Now, she was grieving and anxious to do whatever she could to help.

Johnia Berry's death stunned viewers across East Tennessee. The stunningly beautiful college student who grew up in the Tri-Cities area had been brutally attacked with no clear motive inside her Knoxville apartment. And somehow, the killer was able to get away.

It was almost Christmas, and Johnia's last act the night she died was to wrap presents for some children who she believed needed some extra love from a friend.

Journalists love to land exclusive interviews, and I was no exception. That day, I knew my reporting would get significant attention. Joan, I was told, would be appealing to the public for help to find Johnia's killer. Back at the newsroom, my editors were waiting for me to return with the evening's lead report.

But as I walked toward the home where Joan waited inside, I was overcome with a sense of dread. I distinctly remember hesitating and getting confused about why I felt that way. I'd spoken to victims and victims' families many times before. But this time, it was different. And then it dawned on me why. Just nine months earlier, I'd become a father for the first time. I couldn't wait to get home and see my son, so the thought of what it must be like to lose a child made me wince with dread at what I was about to encounter.

My friend led us to the living room. There, seated on a couch by the fireplace, was a woman whose beauty and elegance immediately reminded me of Johnia, whose photos had splashed across local news headlines for days. Then, I looked into Joan's eyes, and to this day, what I saw still haunts me.

Attempting to muster the strength to stand and greet me was the embodiment of horror, the living expression of terror and grief and rage. It was the face of someone who was enduring the worst imaginable nightmare.

For the next hour, Joan braced against waves of emotion and talked about her beloved little girl, about the nightmare of seeing her wounded body at the funeral home and the desperate need for information that would lead police to her killer. Two decades later, I can still recall in detail Joan's description of standing by the casket and cleaning Johnia's fingernails before the funeral service, a final act of an adoring mother's love.

Joan had come home to Northeast Tennessee on a mission—a mission she would have given anything to avoid—because of a reality she would have given anything to undo. But if it could help find Johnia's killer, Joan was willing to do it, even if it meant talking to me with a news camera recording it all.

Joan's courage paid off. Soon, Johnia's picture appeared on billboards and tractor-trailers across Tennessee appealing for tips to find her killer. That process took years and countless more interviews. Along the way, Joan became an advocate for DNA testing of suspected violent criminals—and she didn't just talk to reporters. Joan demanded the attention of state lawmakers who found it hard to ignore the pleadings of a grieving mother whose story illustrated gaping holes in the laws governing victim rights. Joan, the terror-filled mother, turned out to be a force to be reckoned with.

But it wasn't all about finding the killer or changing the law. One day, Joan called me to ask a question: Would I help get the word out about a toy drive in Johnia's memory?

The night of the attack, Johnia was wrapping Christmas gifts for kids she knew who needed encouragement. Joan was going to finish the job in Johnia's memory for as many needy children as possible. It marked the birth of the Johnia Berry Holiday Toy Drive which continues to be an annual blessing to hundreds of children across Northeast Tennessee and Southwest Virginia.

Time has given me the chance to see Joan's smile, something that seemed unlikely on that cold winter day when we first met. Now, every visit with Joan comes with the warmest hug and the encouraging words of gratitude for getting out the word about the toy drive or her advocacy work for victims. Her face is still beautiful, just like Johnia's in the photos of the brilliant young woman frozen forever in time. But even after all these years, Joan's pain is still palpable when you meet her. In a way that's hard to describe, it's the reality that greets her when she wakes up and stands by her bedside as she drifts off to sleep.

I'm forever grateful to have met Joan Berry and witnessed her fight to stop a cruel killer from getting the final word and to make sure that the name and legacy of Johnia Berry will live on forever.

Josh Smith, *former TV journalist/broadcaster*

Part One

December 6, 2004

On a cold, rainy morning, my ringing cell phone startled me awake. I noticed it was very early in the morning as I grabbed the phone off the bedside table and answered it.

An unfamiliar voice asked to speak to my husband, Mike Berry.

"This is his wife, Joan Berry. This is my cell phone. Can I help you?"

The stranger insisted on speaking with my husband. "Please. It's important," he told me.

The loud ringing had disturbed Mike's sleep, and he was already sitting up on his side of the bed. I handed him the phone.

"Hello?" He slumped over, and I knew something was terribly wrong when he shouted, "Who is this? I need to speak with someone in charge!"

I jumped out of bed. "What's wrong? What happened?"

I kept trying to get him to tell me what was going on until he moved to the other room to continue his call. "Call your sister!" I heard him say.

My sister lived in Bluff City, Tennessee. When she was on the line, Mike asked to speak with her.

"Hello, Patti. We just received a call from someone at UT Hospital, and they said they had a young lady there that was a victim of a break-in, and they believe she's our daughter. They need someone to identify the body!"

I don't know how my legs had the power to move, but I remember running downstairs. For what, I don't know.

Midway down the steps, I fell on my knees, pressing my face into my hands and begging God. "Please don't let it be true!"

I was too hysterical to think about calling Johnia's cell phone. All Mike and I wanted to do was to get to Johnia as fast as possible. We threw on our clothes and put the dog in the car, having no time to make other arrangements for her. It may have only been a four-hour drive from Atlanta, Georgia, to the University of Tennessee Hospital in Knoxville, Tennessee, but it was the longest ride of my life.

Mike drove while I called Tim and Kelly, our sons and Johnia's older brothers. Tim was in Bristol, and Kelly lived in Knoxville, so they were closer to the hospital than us. I cried hysterically as I spoke to them. "It's Johnia! She's at UT Hospital. You need to get there as soon as possible!" I couldn't bear to think of my sweet girl alone. "I'm so sorry. It's not good!"

Time went by as the scenery on the interstate whizzed past us. I could think of nothing but Johnia.

"It must be true!" I cried. "It must be Johnia, or the boys would have called us by now."

As if hearing my words, the skies opened up, and it rained all the way to Knoxville. It's as if the angels were crying.

When we finally pulled into the parking lot at the UT Hospital, Patti, Kelly, and Tim were already there. They had been waiting for us with other family members for a couple of hours. I spotted my son, Kelly, in the parking lot.

I jumped out of the car with my heart in my hands and ran to him. "Is it true? Is it Johnia?"

Kelly had been standing sentinel, ready to deliver the news. "Yes, Mom. Yes, it's Johnia."

I fell into his arms as my grief overtook me. My darling daughter, my baby, was gone, and my life was changed forever.

Johnia's Life

Johnia (pronounced *John-A*) Hope Berry was born on a sunny Friday morning on August 26, 1983, in Russell County, Virginia. She weighed seven pounds, eight ounces, and I was overwhelmed by her beautiful strawberry-blonde hair and hazel eyes.

How do you describe your emotions upon seeing your child? Johnia was as beautiful as the rising sun and filled my heart with love and hope beyond anything I could have ever imagined. She and her brothers were my whole world, and I knew her birth signaled something wonderful.

My heart filled with joy, and I cried the first time I saw her! She was such a pretty baby, and I felt like God had specially blessed me with her.

Her older brothers, Tim and Kelly, beamed over her. They met her in the hospital—and because they were older than her—they were very protective. The boys were delighted about having a baby sister and somewhat amazed. They often said she was such a tiny little thing.

Right away, they were watchful over her. When Johnia was about two and a half, she climbed over the side of her crib, falling and breaking her leg. She had a tiny little white cast on her leg. Her brothers were really upset—especially Tim.

I felt so very bad about her fall. I worried that people would think she had been abused. Of course, that wasn't the case, and our family and friends knew we adored her, but every now and then, when I looked at the cast, tears would well in my eyes, and I wished I could reverse time and save Johnia from the painful fall.

Looking back, I'm amazed at how fast she grew!

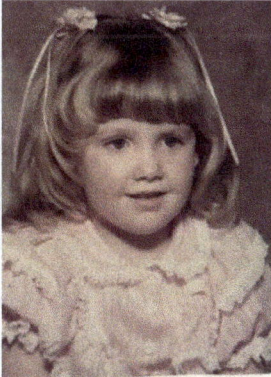

Johnia Hope Berry

She was a good baby. Johnia loved Winnie the Pooh, and she collected the VHS movies. Her love for Winnie the Pooh continued into her adult years.

Johnia liked to play around with her brothers. She could chew her toenails and ribbed Tim and Kelly when they couldn't do the same.

She was cooperative, and she didn't cause a lot of trouble. She was respectful to her elders, and some people thought she acted like a little adult.

As a child and into her adulthood, Johnia wanted her door to stay open at night. I could leave it cracked to help muffle some noise, but she didn't like her door closed as she slept. It helped her doze off when she knew someone was within hearing distance.

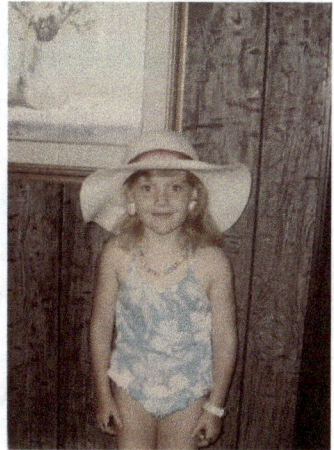

I owned a full-service salon in Abingdon, Virginia, for eighteen years. Occasionally, Johnia would spend time with me there. I had a large lounge in the back, and she would watch movies and play with her ponies and dolls. She loved having her little fingernails and toenails painted at the shop. She'd hold her small fingers in the nail dryer very carefully and patiently.

Johnia always wrote little notes to her family members. Sometimes, she left letters for her dad and called him "Mikey". Everyone treasured her special writings, and we saved several of them. I'm so glad we have them!

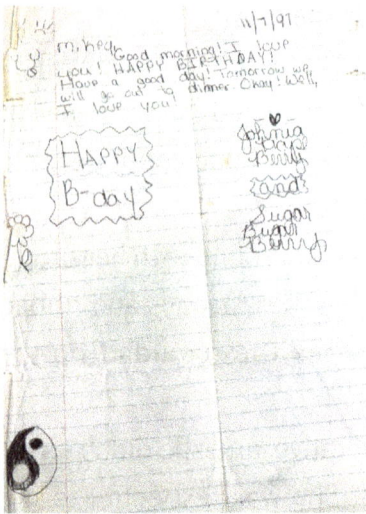

Johnia's note to her dad. "Mikey" was her nickname for him.

The sweet papers said basically the same thing to everyone:

I love you. I hope you love me. From: HOPIE

Before long, she was ready for kindergarten. She had just turned five years old when she started school at Oak Grove Elementary School, and I was concerned because she was younger than all the other children in her class. I shouldn't have worried, though, as Johnia was energetic in class, and she loved going to school from the first day. She was so smart, and her intelligence shined through in all her subjects.

We moved to a different school district in the middle of her kindergarten year. However, she finished kindergarten before changing schools. She started her first grade school year at Holston View Elementary School in Bristol, Tennessee.

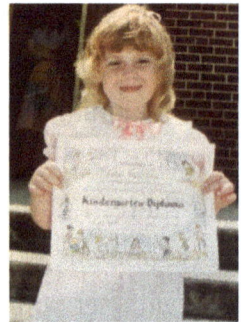

In elementary school, she decided she wanted to be called by her middle name, Hope, because people couldn't say *Johnia* correctly. Many people called her *Jon-e-a* by mistake. Even though introducing herself as "Hope" helped people annunciate her name, Johnia only went by her middle name for a short time.

Johnia's youth was filled with a rainbow of My Little Ponies, and she liked Care Bears, Winnie-the-Pooh, Barbie dolls, and Girl

Scouts. She was proud to be a Brownie Scout in her Girl Scout Troop! She was happy to participate in all the meetings and she sold her share of Girl Scout cookies.

She had all the stuffed characters in the Pooh show. Eeyore was one of her favorites, and his tail was removable and replaceable. As an adult, she took Eeyore with her when she left home for college.

Her favorite color was pink, but she liked purple, too! She wore a lot of pink and purple clothes.

In second grade, Johnia got her first pet, a white terrier dog she named "Sugar". She liked to put Sugar in little dresses, and her favorite outfit was a little pink tutu, but it was probably because Johnia had a pink tutu, too!

Johnia loved to dress Sugar in her doll clothes and put ribbons on her ears. Once, we painted Sugar's nails! Of course, I helped with it, and you know they had to be pink!

Johnia started dancing when she was in elementary school. She did ballet, tap, jazz, and acrobatics. I loved to watch her movements, and I was proud to be present at her recitals.

A Special Painting

A very sweet lady offered to paint a portrait of Johnia when she was eight years old. At the time, I owned my own salon, so I traded the services there as payment for the piece.

Dottie French took the time to visit our home and select Johnia's dress. She removed the mirror from the wall and placed Johnia in front of it, setting the scene carefully. Johnia played with my pearl necklace as Dottie sketched her.

The painting is a sight to behold, and it is one of my most treasured material possessions. It's a beautiful moment captured in time, preserving one small part of my beloved daughter.

Middle Years

Johnia attended Vance Middle School. Her teachers were impressed with her scholastic aptitude and complimented her frequently.

In fact, one of her teachers wrote a letter after Johnia passed away. Johnia loved her sixth-grade teacher, and it seemed the feeling was mutual.

Carol Perkins sent a letter about Johnia that spoke to my heart. I am so fortunate Johnia's educators loved my sweet daughter and saw her potential.

"She brought JOY to so many people! I remember her sitting in the front row of my sixth-grade classroom at Holston View Elementary School in Bristol, Tennessee. Her smile and willingness to participate always encouraged my teaching. One of her many admirable qualities was her

compassion and desire to help others, whether it be fellow classmates, friends, teachers-but especially children!

While at Tennessee High School, she became my student assistant, who guided students with an enthusiastic, positive attitude. Her efficient organizational skills really benefitted our classroom.

How proud I was when I learned her educational and lifelong goal was to help children! What a difference Johnia made, and could have continued to make, in the future!

My memories are many, such as her excitement while sharing pictures of her prom dress, taking dance classes with Kristen and Becky, and her sweet hugs as she shared the news about her engagement the last time I saw her. I am forever grateful for being her teacher and friend and will cherish these fond memories forever!" —**Carol Perkins**

In middle school, Johnia had lots of friends, but she had several close friends she spent more time with than others. She also had friends from the dance studio and Top Gun Cheerleading.

Johnia had sleepovers often, and we usually took one of her close friends on vacations and shopping trips. It seems like there was always something going on, from banquets to dances and cheer competitions.

Johnia and I were busy, but we were happy. Our family continued to get closer, and Johnia's compassionate personality grew.

The material in school got harder, but Johnia rose to the challenge. She became a model student and developed wonderful study habits that she carried into higher levels of learning.

Johnia started dancing at Watt's Dance Studio in 1992. She truly enjoyed it and danced with them until 2001, when she graduated high school.

Johnia enjoyed cheerleading. She started in 1996 when she was in the seventh grade.

My daughter played softball for a short time. She quickly decided to pursue her other interests.

Johnia was in the Cotillion. A Cotillion is an etiquette class for students in middle school. A teacher or teachers attempt to mold young boys and girls into charming young ladies and men through formal and informal dances. Additional etiquette classes may provide perspective about acceptable behavior during dinners and special events.

She really enjoyed the etiquette classes and the dance. She loved dressing up!

The father and daughter dance was special for Johnia and her dad. I loved seeing my husband and our daughter have so much fun together. Her dad even took some dance classes just for her!

Johnia was a member of the Junior Beta Club, and she received the Good Citizenship Award. She seemed to like staying busy and was very intelligent.

Some of her favorite movies were The Secret Garden and Dirty Dancing. We watched them many times together!

Holidays were always exciting for Johnia, and she loved them all! Christmas was her favorite time of year. She had her very own tree in her bedroom. She and I decorated it with ballet ornaments, shiny tinsel, and beautiful stars.

Her dance team always performed in the Christmas Parade in Bristol. The temperature was freezing, but it was so much fun for all the girls. One year I heard the Christmas song, *All I Want for Christmas is You*, by Mariah Carey so many times that I knew every single word. I thank God for these precious memories!

High School

Johnia started school at Tennessee High School in August 1998. She maintained academic excellence and earned awards from the National Beta Club and National Honor Society.

Johnia pursued psychology and social sciences. She was fascinated by the human mind, and she enjoyed helping others.

Becky Bowman and Lacey Pope were her best friends. They visited the house often, spending the night, watching movies, and just having fun being together.

Johnia loved cheerleading, and she shook her pom-poms throughout high school. Johnia was a varsity cheerleader at Tennesse High, and she cheered with Top Gun Acad-

emy. Top Gun was considered competitive cheerleading, and we traveled to many states for competition.

Johnia danced at Watt's Dance Studio until she graduated high school. She learned ballet, jazz, and tap dancing. What great memories we have of the dance recitals, and all the costumes were so much fun for Johnia and all the girls!

Her dance team danced at Disney World and on a cruise ship. Johnia met a nice young man, Stephen Morgan, on the cruise. They became good friends and dated for a while.

Stephen lived in Asheville, North Carolina, but he would visit Johnia often. They dated for about a year but remained friends through their college years. Stephen attended ETSU when Johnia was there.

Their senior proms were on the same day! Of course, Stephen invited Johnia to his prom. It was a tough decision for Johnia, but she gave up her senior prom with her friends to go to Stephen's prom.

The venue was the Biltmore Estate in Asheville, North Carolina. Can you imagine? Johnia must have felt like royalty as she approached the beautiful mansion George Vanderbilt constructed.

She and I shopped for weeks looking for a special dress. I have to say, we found the perfect one! Of all the purple prom dresses in the world, the one Johnia wore to her prom was my favorite! My daughter looked absolutely gorgeous, and Steven was quite handsome.

They had a great time and got to meet Justin Timberlake! Johnia was beside herself with excitement!

Johnia's first car was a red Chrysler Sebring Convertible. It was a great car, and she had a lot of fun times in it!

It seemed like we blinked, and it was time for her to graduate high school. It definitely flew by too quickly.

On the Sunday before she graduated, we attended a baccalaureate service at Tennessee High.

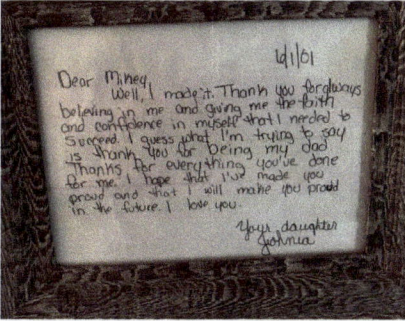

Johnia graduated with honors in June 2001. On a sunny day, she accepted her honors degree along with an Academic Performance Scholarship. Her dad, her brothers, and I were so proud of her!

To celebrate her achievement, we threw a party for her. The house was full of family and friends who were all happy to congratulate Johnia on her high school graduation.

Johnia appreciated the time her father and I took to support her in her extracurricular activities. Unlike some teens, Johnia seemed to like spending time with her parents, and we were happy that she felt like she could talk to us about anything.

She flew to Cancun for a graduation trip with her girlfriends. It was an exciting graduation trip for the girls! One of her friends became ill, and Johnia called to ask her dad and me if there were medicines she should get for her. She was always more concerned about the health and happiness of others than she was about having fun.

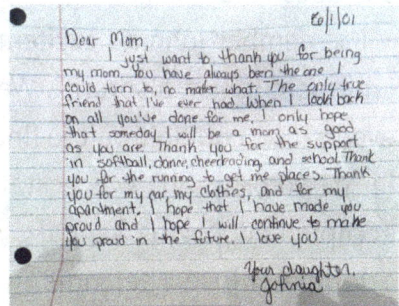

Johnia's letter upon graduating high school.

Johnia in Cancun.

College

Johnia entered East Tennessee State University in 2001, pursuing a major in Child Psychology with a minor in Criminal Justice and Criminology. In college, Johnia's bubbly personality was infectious, earning her the "Tigger" nickname, the comparison clearly related to a character from the well-loved A.A. Milne tale.

Some people told me Johnia was an overachiever. I replied, "Well, she doesn't let the grass grow under her feet."

I remember Johnia's excitement when she signed up during recruitment to join a sorority. We paid the fee, and she attended the events. She couldn't wait to find out if she had gained membership in the sorority. She was ecstatic when she learned she had been accepted into Sigma Kappa!

Johnia enjoyed her time in Sigma Kappa and quickly formed strong bonds with the young ladies in the organization. During her initiation, she met her friend and sorority mentor, Jocelyn Mooneyhan. Jocelyn has been married since shortly after her college graduation, and she and I speak frequently.

Jocelyn's relationship with Johnia began as her "Inspirational Sister/Guardian Angel"—a title Jocelyn took seriously. Soon, the pair were good friends.

In the fall of 2001, Johnia was a freshman at the university, and Jocelyn was a senior. She was assigned to her as a sorority mentor, and during Johnia's initiation week, Jocelyn left her notes and gifts related to their sorority's theme for their induction week.

Jocelyn recalled happy times with Johnia, recounting a specific springtime outing in Johnia's Chrysler Sebring convertible. Phil Collins's song "Something Happened on the Way to Heaven" played while they were out, and for some reason, even before Johnia's death, the song stuck in Jocelyn's mind when she thought about their beautiful drive.

From left: Johnia and Jocelyn Mooneyhan Lacey

Jocelyn has bittersweet memories of Johnia, as her happy recollections are tinged with the sadness of Johnia's death. Her only regret is that she didn't have the chance to know her friend longer.

Sigma Kappa's symbols include doves, hearts, and violets. Their emblems stand out to Jocelyn when she remembers Johnia and her time in the sorority.

Jocelyn often thinks about her time with Johnia and relates it to a song by The Band Perry, a group from Greenville, Tennesse, who received some fame for their song titled "If I Die Young". For those familiar with the lyrics of the song, it evokes images of a young woman who passes before her time and wishes to be remembered fondly, even though her experiences in life were cut short. She asks that those who dress her for her funeral place pearls around her neck and speaks of the "Ballad of the Dove" which evokes feelings of "peace and love."

Jocelyn said, "The song conjures up memories surrounding Johnia's death, as the lyrics were so similar to her story. Johnia died young, she was stabbed repeatedly with a knife, and she was engaged to be married, leaving behind a young man devastated by her death.

"On a personal level, I felt my sorority bond with Johnia even more because a couple of the lyrics mentioned one of our sorority's national symbols (the dove) and our sorority jewel (the pearl)."

Jocelyn went on to say, "On the second anniversary of Johnia's death, and with Johnia's killer still at large, Joan asked me to speak at a vigil at Johnia's grave in the hopes that the media attention would have someone come forward to give police information on who killed Johnia. One of the things I said is that I considered the day Johnia died as her birthday in Heaven. We all have an earthly birthday, the day we physically came into the world. Johnia's earthly birthday is August twenty-sixth, and her heavenly birthday is December sixth, the day she entered Heaven's gates and met her Lord and Savior."

Johnia had always loved babysitting for friends and teachers, and she continued helping children at East Tennessee State University's Child Study Center. Johnia spent three and a half years with the school's early learning program. The children adored her, and Johnia's coworkers only had good things to say about her.

While at ETSU, Johnia was involved in a work-study program at Woodridge Hospital in Johnson City, Tennessee. The facility provided mental health and co-occurring substance use disorders for adults and adolescents. Her work there was with adolescents.

Johnia was on the dean's list, in the Psi Chi Honor Society, and inducted into the Sigma Kappa Sorority. She would have graduated early with a 3.78 grade point average.

Whenever Johnia would come home from college for a visit, she would always yell as soon as she got through the door, "I'm home, family!"

How I loved to hear her spirited voice! It always made me so happy. I could feel the sincere love she had in her heart for her family and her excitement about being at home. We always welcomed her with big smiles and hugs!

Johnia's Convertible Car

Johnia came home from college for a long visit. She convinced her dad that she needed a new car. Looking back, I don't think I really knew he was serious about getting her a new car.

They went car shopping one afternoon, and they brought a very small two-seater convertible sports car home for me to see. It was actually a very sharp-looking car and fun to drive.

I think I put a little damper on that car when I told Johnia that the car was too small, and she wouldn't be able to put her shoes in the car or get her clothes in it when she traveled.

Mike Berry in Johnia's car

On February 10, 2003, they brought home another car. It was a red 2003 Mitsubishi Eclipse Spyder Convertible with a black top. This time, they purchased the car before they brought it home for my approval. Of course, I loved it, and I was happy to see Johnia in her new vehicle.

Mikey said it was an early Valentine's Day gift, and Johnia was beside herself with excitement!

Shortly after she got the car, we went shopping and the weather was still very chilly. Johnia loved riding with the top down on her car, but she hadn't been able to do it often because the weather had been cold since she'd gotten it. So, that day we put the top down with the windows up and turned the heater on!

It started to rain so we had to stop and put the top up. We had a few minutes of the wind through our hair, though.

During another shopping trip, we decided to take Johnia's car.

Johnia loved animal print. She decorated her space with it.

We found a chair wrapped in cheetah print. Some people may remember the tall high-heeled chairs of the early 2000s. Well, this was one of those chairs—tall, in style, and cheetah-printed.

Johnia saw it first and rushed over to it yelling, "Look, Mom, look!"

We tried it out, and I was surprised that the chair was comfortable. With its unique design, I could tell it was going to be a conversation piece.

Johnia really wanted the chair, so without a thought about how we were going to get it back to her apartment, we bought it. Of course, that particular piece of furniture wouldn't have fit in the trunk of her car, so we put the top down and stuck it into her backseat.

Down the road we went, with a cheetah print high heel jutting from the car. I don't know what people thought when they saw us, but we had a great time!

Just Before Graduate School

Remembered as Tennessee's first capitol and the Marble City for its marble-filled quarries, Knoxville is the home to over 190,740 residents. When Johnia moved into Brendon Park Apartments in October 2004, she didn't know she would never have the chance to see the full bloom of the dogwoods in the spring or go to her first graduate class.

I had no idea that several unhappy residents had posted about the lack of security and frequent vandalism at her apartment complex. I visited her and stayed the night in the apartment, and I hoped she was safe.

Johnia had applied to pursue a master's degree in psychology and had been accepted to the University of Tennessee in Knoxville. She was on track to graduate from East Tennessee State University in the middle of December and begin her classes at UT Knoxville in January.

Johnia's roommate was her best friend's ex-boyfriend, Jason Aymami, whom she had met while attending East Tennessee State University. She decided to share the apartment with him until she could find other accommodations.

She had lived with her fiancé, Jason White, in Lansing, Michigan, while they attended Thomas Cooley Law School. At the time, Johnia was the youngest female admitted to the program, but she realized she would rather work with children. They shared an apartment for a couple of months before she left for Knoxville. Her friend's ex-boyfriend offered to let her have an empty room in his apartment while she searched for a place of her own.

The separation was hard on Johnia and Jason, who were very much in love. They spoke to each other every night until Johnia fell asleep. When she no longer answered him, Jason would hang up.

Johnia worked at Zales Jewelry Store in the West Town Mall, and the employees and manager spoke highly of her. She remained cheerful, even when customers were rude or "hit on" her. On the evening before her murder, a co-worker walked her to her car, and they spoke for a quarter of an hour. He noted a suspicious man driving around them, but Johnia's trusting nature made her oblivious to the strange man and his odd action.

Johnia also spent time in a work-study program at Peninsula Hospital as a psychiatric technician. She worked with children and adolescents who were delinquent, mentally troubled, or whose home lives were intolerable. Johnia enjoyed her time with the youth. She helped them by playing games and interacting in counseling sessions.

Johnia missed Jason, but she was living a fulfilling life. She was looking forward to her early undergraduate graduation, her graduate studies, and her wedding scheduled for April.

Unfortunately, she never saw any of those special events.

Johnia and Jason

Every young woman hopes for a beautiful love story. My daughter had one.

Johnia met Jason White in the fall of 2001 when they both were attending East Tennessee State University. I remember how excited she was when she told me about Jason, and she couldn't wait for her dad and me to meet him!

I recall her saying, "You guys could come after work one evening this week for a quick meet." We were happy to take her up on the offer.

Johnia and Jason White

Mike and I met them at Wendy's fast-food restaurant in Gray, Tennessee, which was only about fifteen or twenty minutes from their college. Jason was quite handsome, with sandy blond hair and the sweetest smile, but he was a little on the quiet side. Johnia kept the conversation going, though! It was a short meeting that evening, but it didn't take long for Jason to become part of our family life.

Johnia and Jason spent lots of time together. When Johnia came home to Atlanta, Georgia, for visits, she loved to bring Jason along. Jason was part of our family vacations, beach trips, and our family Christmases.

Our family loved Jason almost as much as Johnia loved him. I thought his multiple proposals were beautiful, and he treated my daughter with the love and respect I'd always hoped she'd find when she got involved with someone special to her.

Johnia enjoyed spending time with Jason's family, too, especially in the summer when she relaxed at their pool. She talked about going with his family on annual trips to the mountains.

Johnia developed a special relationship with Jason's mother, Norma. Johnia told me that when she and Norma went shopping together, people thought the two of them were sisters and sometimes mother and daughter. She thought that was pretty cool!

Christmas 2003 was a special Christmas for Johnia and Jason. As usual, we had our family Christmas at my sister's, Patti's, old country farmhouse, as it was reserved for special times for our family.

It was always beautiful and festive. My sister collected antique furniture and decorated the house with vintage Christmas decorations. The Christmas tree and the fire crackling made it feel cozy and inviting, and the people who attended the events there filled it with love and happiness.

In 2003, Mike and I made the trip from Atlanta to Bluff City, Tennessee, and we were the last ones to arrive. Johnia and Jason were already there and everyone was enjoying each other's company.

Johnia was so excited to see us and couldn't wait to share the gift Jason had given her for Christmas! A RING! AN ENGAGEMENT RING!! A BEAUTIFUL, PRINCESS CUT DIAMOND RING. Johnia's happiness could not be contained.

That was the last family Christmas we spent at the old farmhouse, and there have been so many changes since that Christmas. Two of the most tragic events to hit our family were Johnia's murder and Josey, my sister's youngest son, lost his life in an accident. In addition, my mom and dad have passed away. Now, the grandchildren have grown up and are in college in different states.

After Johnia and Jason's engagement, there was a lot of talking and planning for a wedding. We looked at various venues and discussed the colors for the bridesmaid's dresses. Johnia tried on wedding gowns, and she checked with Jason about the guest list. Everything most young women think to plan for their special day, like food and music, was planned.

My daughter's dream wedding and her marriage with the man she loved were stolen. This wonderful young woman who had love, hopes, and dreams was senselessly murdered!

I kept the beautiful wedding gown that Johnia never got to wear. *How could I part with it?* Four beautiful bridesmaid's dresses and the other things Johnia had purchased for her wedding remain untouched. They wait for the precious young lady who never got to have her special day.

Jason wanted Johnia to be buried in her engagement ring. At the time of her funeral, many of Johnia's belongings were still held at the Knox County Sheriff's Office. We asked, and they returned the ring. Before her funeral, during his time alone with her, Jason placed the ring on Johnia's finger for the final time.

"Dreaming of You" by Selena was a special song for Johnia and Jason. It was supposed to play at their wedding as they danced. Instead, Jason asked the funeral director to play the song at Johnia's funeral.

Johnia had asked her brother, Kelly, to play the piano at her wedding. Since that would never take place, he played for her at her funeral. The song wasn't titled, as he simply played from his heart. I dare say the song would have been different if he wouldn't have played it through his grief.

During the Christmas of 2004, Johnia worked part-time at Zales Jewelry in West Town Mall. The manager told us that Johnia had chosen a wedding band for Jason, and she was holding it for her.

Mike and I bought the ring. Nineteen years later, Johnia's dad, my husband, still wears that ring.

On the night Johnia was murdered, she fell asleep talking to Jason. It wasn't uncommon for them. They loved each other so much, and since they couldn't be together, they fell asleep to the sound of their voices.

I am thankful for the many wonderful memories of Johnia and Jason's relationship. I'm so glad that she found a special love with Jason and was able to experience

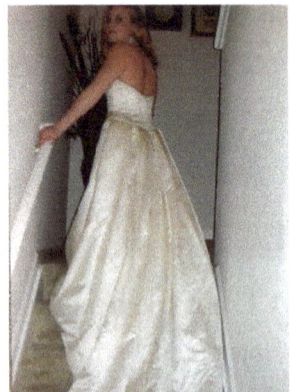

all the happiness that comes along with it. Oh, how my heart hurts for the loss of my precious daughter and the things that were taken from her!

Jason's mother, Norma, had some thoughts about Johnia and the time she spent with their family. I will share her words.

"Jason first met Johnia when she was a cheerleader at ETSU. One of Jason's friends—who was a guy cheerleader—asked him if he wanted to meet some cheerleaders. Jason said, "Yes, as long as they aren't a bunch of guys."

Jason told me Johnia was so sweet and friendly, and not stuck-up.

You asked me about sweet stories. Jason and Johnia would sit on our couch with a blanket and pick out names for their children. A boy would be Cody, and they'd name a girl Isabella.

When I went with Johnia to her doctor's appointment, a nurse said to me in front of Johnia, "You have to be her mother. She looks just like you." We were told that a lot by Jason's friends.

Johnia would often stop by with a child she was caring for. She just loved kids. They would swim in our pool.

Sometimes, when Johnia would stop by, Lee and I would be getting ready to go somewhere, and Johnia would jump in the car with us. She stayed with us during the summer before she went to law school. She missed Jason so much while he was in Michigan.

Johnia had a full class schedule at ETSU, and we were at work and doing a full remodel of the kitchen. We had a lot of grilled cookout food because the kitchen was a mess. Johnia never complained. One

evening, Johnia said in a really sweet voice, "Do we have to have cook-out food again?" I think we ordered a pizza that night.

Mostly, I remember Johnia was patient. I remember small conversations with her. She got to meet both my dad and my mom. My dad stayed one weekend when she and Jason were here. He lived in Williamsburg, Virginia. My Dad just loved Johnia. My mom and her sister, who was visiting from Maryland, came to our house and Johnia did one of her quick visits. I'm so glad she did. It was the last time I ever saw her, and I have a picture of her, my mom, and my aunt that day sitting on my dresser.

One more thing. When we all went to Michigan to move Jason to law school, my husband, Lee, was a wreck. He looked at the apartment building, all the snow, and the town, and he wanted to drive Jason home. It was Johnia and me that pulled together as a team to help Lee and Jason. They were both depressed. Johnia and I cleaned the apartment, hung pictures, and made it look like a home. When Lee and I had to leave after two days, Johnia stayed with Jason for about two weeks. Jason found out he needed a suit for something at school, so Johnia went to a thrift store and found one for him.

You always share a sweet picture that they got taken on New Year's Eve. Jason wouldn't have made it during those first weeks of law school if it had not been for Johnia helping him in Michigan. She was his rock."

I reached out to Jason, and he provided a few memories from the time he shared with Johnia.

"My relationship with Johnia began with a chance encounter through a mutual friend. My neighbor, Josh, was a male cheerleader for East

Tennessee State University. You know, the kind of male cheerleader that throws the other ones in the air to provide the muscle for those high-flying maneuvers. One Friday night, Josh stopped in for a visit.

"'I'm going to a party with some cheerleaders later, you wanna tag along,' Josh offered.

"'Is it a party for other male cheerleaders, or will there actually be some females there?' I asked.

"'There's going to be plenty of girls there, you should come,' Josh replied.

"So, I went to the party and one of the female cheerleaders present was Johnia. It wasn't exactly love at first sight—at least for Johnia. In fact, by the end of the night, Johnia ended up throwing me out of her apartment for lighting a cigarette indoors. It seemed an unlikely romance.

"A few weeks later, I ran into Johnia on campus. I made amends for the cigarette incident, and Johnia apologized for overreacting and throwing me out. She told me that it was her birthday, and I volunteered to take her to lunch. She accepted. From there, numbers were exchanged and future plans to meet again were decided.

"What ensued was quite simply, new love. Exquisite, inspiring, opulent, untouchable love. The type of love that makes all those movies, books, and songs suddenly make sense. This was what it was all about. After a year or so, I bought an engagement ring and asked Johnia to marry me. Johnia accepted the proposal but just one proposal was not enough.

"For the next few months, Johnia insisted that I propose to her multiple times in various public places as was her bubbly and effervescent per-sonality. She wanted to hold onto those feelings. She wanted to re-live them and savor them. She wanted to love and be excited about being loved and then she wanted to rewind the tape and play it all over again. And each proposal seemed just as exciting for her as the first. It never seemed to get old for her. I ended up proposing at half a dozen locations around campus, a few retail stores, during a rafting trip, a public park, and finally at a family dinner over the holidays where everyone else in the family finally became aware.

"To lose Johnia was a devastating blow for me. There are many different kinds of death—just as there are many different kinds of love. The loss of an elderly grandparent is very different from the loss of a child, which in turn, is very different from the loss of significant other.

"Johnia and I were very much at the pinnacle of new love at the time of her death. Those feelings were new, exciting, promising, and very comforting. To have that ripped away in a sudden and violent way felt like multiple tragedies befalling me at once. It was the loss of a relationship, but it was also the death of all our dreams together. The children, first house, honeymoon, anniversaries, graduations, birthdays, and every other major life milestone we may have experienced together was suddenly and inexplicably yanked away.

"At the time of Johnia's death, I was in my third semester of law school. I had a loving fiancé, my children's names picked out, and I was laying the groundwork for a long, happy life with Johnia. I was in the top ten percent of my law school class before Johnia died.

"Following her death, I took a leave of absence from law school. When I returned, I was a different person. I was no longer at the top of my class. I was distracted, withdrawn, and grieving. I went from being an A+ student to a C+ student. I struggled with the remainder of law school, and my struggle was understandable. I was attending law school to learn about the justice system. To have to sit and listen to hypothetical lectures about justice while going through the stark, cold reality of a painful injustice was difficult, to say the least. It was like watching your house burn down only to have the fire department show up and give you a quiz on how great the fire department is.

"In the years that followed, I eventually graduated from law school and passed the bar exam. Feats that seemed average but truly were amazing given my circumstances. There are plenty of students who fail those goals with much less mental anguish and adversity.

"My first job as an attorney was serving as Assistant Attorney General for the State of Florida. My job duties—litigating against convicted criminals on behalf of the Florida Department of Corrections. No big surprise where the inspiration for that job came from. I built a career out of inmate litigation at the federal level.

"Today, I am an Attorney Advisor for the Federal Bureau of Prisons. How do I feel when I'm involved in a legal case with someone like Johnia's murderer? Does it re-open a wound? Is it cathartic? Has it helped evolve my outlook on the justice system? It's certainly a complicated profession for me.

"When the killer was arrested, the media interviewed me and asked me what I would say if I was face-to-face with him.

"My reply was, 'I'd tell him that I experienced more freedom on my lunch break today than he will experience for the rest of his life.' A prediction that turned out to be all too accurate.

"I struggled with relationships for the next several years following Johnia's death. Partly due to the grief I endured at her loss and partly due to the fact it was hard to replicate my first true love in another relationship. Her memory has always colored my perspective and I will carry it with me for the rest of my life.

"What death has taught me is that everyone handles it differently, and it doesn't always make sense."

What is Jason doing now?

Jason White is a U.S. Department of Justice attorney who represents the Federal Bureau of Prisons. He is a former assistant attorney general for the State of Florida and a former prosecutor for the Florida Department of Business. Jason graduated from the Florida State University College of Law and East Tennessee State University. He is an avid marksman and outdoors enthusiast, having once participated in the History Channel series, *Top Shot*. Jason is the author of *The Medical Loophole* and enjoys traveling and kickboxing.

He never married.

Part Two

What Happened to Johnia?

December 5, 2004

Johnia worked at the jewelry store and stopped at Walgreens to pick up a few gifts. I talked to her while she was in the store, reminding her she needed to rest to prepare for her early morning. Later, the police confirmed that they had seen footage of her as she spoke on the phone while checking out. Johnia's apartment was a short drive away, and she went home to wrap the presents she had purchased.

Jason, her roommate, arrived home shortly, and they watched television before retiring to their respective rooms.

Some people believe a man and woman cannot live together without a romantic entanglement, but in this case, those individuals would be wrong. Jason Aymami and Johnia were friends and roommates and nothing more. Johnia was devoted to her fiancé and focused on her education, and anyone who knew her, understood that she was living there out of convenience while she looked for her own apartment.

Once in her bedroom, Johnia lay down and called her fiancé around eleven-thirty for their nightly chat. She drifted off to sleep with him on the line, and he ended the call without knowing that it was the last time he'd ever speak to Johnia.

Jason Aymami went to his bedroom around twelve-thirty and fell asleep with the television on. Around three and a half hours later, Jason woke up, startled by a scream.

December 6, 2004

Around four o'clock in the morning, someone opened the door of Johnia's apartment and crept inside. Johnia never wanted her bedroom door closed, so the intruder noticed her open door and slipped into her room.

Johnia woke up and asked the intruder what he was doing, and he told her to "chill out." It's possible that she tried to fight him out of her room, or after waking from a sound sleep, she could have screamed.

For a reason we will never know—other than he was a monster—the perpetrator stabbed Johnia over twenty-five times. She had lacerations on her chest, neck, and face when the criminal left the apartment, leaving a trail of blood behind him.

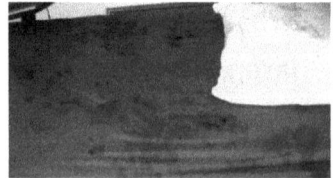

Courtesy of Knox County Sheriff's Department

It's possible that Jason heard my daughter screaming. He dismissed it. He later told reporters that Johnia had nightmares and would cry out. I often wonder what would have happened if he had immediately investigated the sound. *Would he have been able to save my daughter's life?*

Awakened out of a deep sleep, Jason staggered to his door. Upon opening it, he was punched, pushed back on his bed, and stabbed in his chest, arms, and face. He claimed that the attack lasted under a minute, and police learned later that the knife came from the kitchen.

Thank God his television had been on because there was enough light from it to partially see the attacker. The police drew a composite sketch of the man Jason described, and we placed it on a billboard we rented to try to find Johnia's murderer. The short description Jason provided the police was that the man who broke into his apartment was 180 pounds, fair-haired, white, and wearing an Atlanta Braves ball cap.

Jason fought off the intruder, and he bolted out of the apartment. He said that he knocked on the doors of a neighboring apartment complex, but when no one answered, he ran to Weigel's. Weigel's was a half mile away, and there were no other open businesses along the way.

Cammy Walt, assistant manager of Weigel's Farm Store, was there when Jason flew into the store. He was bleeding so heavily that the store had to replace some food items.

The attendant called emergency services. The 9-1-1 call was terrifying.

The attendant explained that Jason was bloody and he looked like he'd been involved in a fight. The operator asked to speak to Jason and he recounted the details of the attack. He asked someone to check on his roommate.

The police responded to the call at 4:14 in the morning. They found Johnia alive.

When Tim and Kelly got to the hospital, Kelly said they were there for a while before they were led to the area where they identified Johnia's body. I'm now —and will always be— upset that the hospital didn't wait until Mike and I arrived to identify Johnia's body.

We were her next of kin! When they asked my boys to identify their sister's body, they inflicted an excruciating, searing pain that my sons will live with for the rest of their lives! Even though they only viewed a photo of Johnia clipped to a board, the memory will be etched into their minds forever.

Her beautiful blonde hair was soaked with blood. That image left an ever-lasting, terrifying picture in their mind of their beautiful sister, who always had an infectious smile.

I only wish that I could have spared them this pain. It saddens my heart that they have to live with such a terrible memory for the rest of their lives.

Neighbors

Johnia awoke to sounds in her room. I don't know what she may have said, but she startled the intruder, and he stabbed her and her roommate multiple times before running out of the apartment. My husband and I learned a few details later, but we don't have the full picture of our daughter's final moments.

What I do know is that my daughter fought for her life.

Courtesy of the Knox County Sheriff's Department

Somehow, after pausing in the living room, my sweet daughter stumbled out of her apartment and into the hall. Her blood was found on all five of her neighbors' doors and in the building's foyer where the police found her. I was devastated to learn that Johnia had tried so hard to find help, but no one had answered their door.

It was early in the morning, but it seemed unlikely that no one heard her knocks and desperate pleas for help. The same people who had seen her in the hallway, maybe exchanging a casual greeting or smiling as she interacted with their children, remained silent while Johnia begged for help.

Johnia was truly a survivor. She was stabbed over twenty times, but she found the strength to try to find help.

Out of all the people who heard her cries, only one of the male occupants called 9-1-1, but he was hesitant to open the door or give a lot of information. He hung up when the dispatcher asked for his name.

Her roommate called for help when he arrived at Weigel's, a local convenience store. Later, he said that he thought he had been the only one attacked, and Johnia had already fled the apartment. Weigle's is a half mile from Brendon Park Apartments, and he claimed he knocked on several doors as he fled. *Why did no one help him? Why did he have to run to the nearest public place before someone called 9-1-1?*

The neighbors were afraid. I understand. *But why couldn't they call emergency services?*

The textbook definition of "neighbor" describes a person who lives within a certain proximity of another person, but I remember thinking of neighbors differently. If someone's house blazed with fire, men, women, and children would bring buckets of water. When I grew up, if a neighbor was attacked, the community would have done anything to help. But now, it's quite the opposite.

It saddens me to think that only one person called 9-1-1 when they heard Johnia pounding on their doors, and that individual hung up before reporting anything. He may have feared for his own life, but what harm would have come to him by staying on the call until emergency services arrived?

I wonder every day if it would have made a difference. My daughter fought for her life, and precious seconds may have saved her.

I have read statements from bystanders who witnessed a violent crime or its result. When asked about the reasons they didn't respond in situations similar to Johnia's case, many people cite that they don't want to get involved in disputes. Additionally, they don't want to go through the trouble of getting called to court to testify.

How sad... And dare I say, selfish.

Sometimes, I wonder if any of her neighbors saw something that night. I hope they didn't feign ignorance when the police questioned them, because it not only violated the law, but it allowed Johnia's murderer to roam free for over two years.

We must all do the right thing and help when we can. It can help stop violence and make the world a safer place.

The day after my precious Johnia lost her life, the people in charge of the apartments posted fliers about her murder. They claimed she had gotten into a fight with her boyfriend, and he had killed her. I couldn't believe my daughter's homicide was being treated as a domestic dispute!

Blood on Johnia's door, leading into the living room

Courtesy of Knox County Sheriff's Department

Even though the police released a statement that confirmed Johnia was not a victim of domestic violence, the management of Brendon Park Apartments never retracted their false information, as many of the tenants tried to break their leases soon after the murder. I was so angry that they were allowed to tarnish her character and there was nothing I could do about it.

My husband and I filed a suit against the apartment complex. The process was too difficult when I had to watch their apathetic reactions to my pleas for them to fix their mistake. In October 2007, it became too much for me to handle, so we settled out of court.

The Last Time I Saw Johnia

Fate can be cruel, and there's never enough time with the ones you love.

The last time my husband and I saw our daughter alive was on Thanksgiving day, November 25, 2004. We went to Bristol for Thanksgiving with the family and then went to Knoxville to have a late Thanksgiving dinner with Johnia, Kelly, and Rachel, Kelly's girlfriend.

Johnia didn't get to have Thanksgiving with the family because she
had to work at Peninsula Hospital.
We had dinner at Calhoun's. I remember how glad I was that we found
a restaurant that was open.

from left: Johnia, mother, and father

When we were leaving that
evening, we all stood in the parking
lot, exchanged hugs, and said how
much we loved each other. Mike and I never in our wildest dreams
thought that was going to be the last time we would ever see our
precious daughter. Each year on Thanksgiving my heart goes back
to that night, and how I love and miss my daughter. I am thankful
for that Thanksgiving, even though it was our last one together.

The picture on the following page was taken at Maggiano's in
Atlanta, Georgia, on Johnia's twenty-first birthday, August 26, 2004.

Johnia Hope Berry
8/26/83 - 12/6/04

Celebration of Johnia's Life

JOHNIA HOPE BERRY
1983 - 2004

Johnia's Celebration of Life took place on Thursday, December ninth, 2004, at eleven o'clock in the morning. The service was held in Bristol, Tennessee, and it was officiated by Reverend John Graham.

Services

CELEBRATION OF LIFE
11 O'Clock Thursday Morning
December 9, 2004
Paul Cook Memorial Chapel
Oakley-Cook Funeral Home
Bristol, Tennessee

OFFICIATING CLERGY
Rev. John Graham

COMMITTAL & INTERMENT
Baker Cemetery
Bluff City, Tennessee

Arrangements especially for Miss Berry
have been made through
OAKLEY-COOK FUNERAL HOME
BRISTOL, TENNESSEE

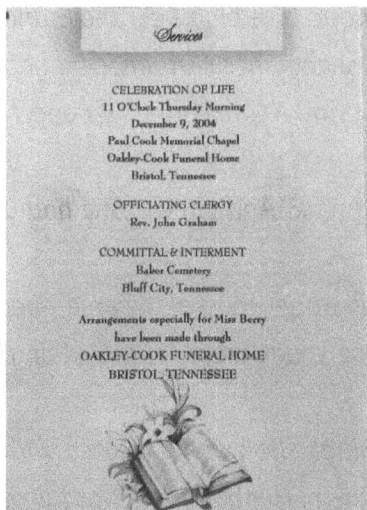

I wasn't the only one who cried that day. Just like on the day she died, the sky shed tears for Johnia.

Several people spoke at my daughter's service. Among them, three of her sorority sisters shared their memories of Johnia.

Ellen Cantrell:

"We come here today as Johnia's friends and sorority sisters to share a few memories of her and celebrate her life. When we think of Johnia, we remember how energetic she was, how she was always bouncing around and wanting to give 110% to everything she did.

At times, we even thought of her as the Energizer Bunny, and at times, we thought we wanted to sit on her so we could calm her down!

She was always a motivator and encouraged us to do things, to try things at least once. She befriended everyone; she didn't care how old you were, or how young you were.

She was always inquisitive. I remember having several classes with her at ETSU and she was always wanting to know what was going on. But she was always that way, with her friends and life in general. Always wanting to know everything. Every little detail. She also wanted to make sure she wasn't missing out on anything. She wanted to know everything."

Kim Taylor:

"One of Johnia's favorite things was leopard print. Her apartment was full of animal print!

She had this big chair. It was in the shape of a high-heel shoe, and it was leopard print. Her comforter, her sheets, her curtains. She had stuffed animals—everything was leopard print! Animal print. Her apartment was full of it!

She also loved wearing pink—anything pink. And purses! She had a purse for every outfit!

With as many purses as she had, she still wore—most of the time—her cheerleader tennis shoes. She loved those shoes more than anything, and she would wear them most of the time.

She was also fascinated with everything! She was fascinated with bubble baths; she couldn't get enough of them! Her bathroom was full of bubble bath and bath salt, and she had tons of makeup and nail polish. And just ask her for anything from her purse and she would have it!

Her purses were huge! She would walk around with her backpack on and her big purses, and you would wonder how she could carry all of it and her dog, too.

She was a true girly girl. She would also come over and make all of us get on the floor—including my sisters—and do ab routines. We would all be out of breath, and she would keep pushing, encouraging us to go. And she was unstoppable!"

Stephanie Wilson:

"Johnia hated being alone. When her roommate wasn't with her, she would come over and hang out with us, so she wouldn't have to be by herself. And she took her dog everywhere!

She took Chiquita to class, took her shopping, and brought her to hang out with us. She took her everywhere!

And she carried her around in her purse. And, you know how people say pets resemble their owners? Well, that dog has as much energy as

Johnia did. Chiquita ran around in circles, and she literally just took her everywhere.

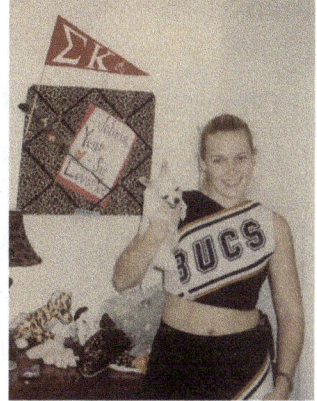

Johnia and Chiquita

And Johnia loved to give people hugs! And it didn't matter if she just met you, she would give you a hug anyway. She always made us feel so special and important!

She was a beautiful, loving, caring girl, and a great friend, and we will miss her very much."

The words from each woman touched my heart and reminded me of the precious influence my sweet daughter had over so many lives. She was a shining light, and no one could extinguish the flame of her memory, even after she was gone.

Death is not the end for those of us who believe in Jesus, and I know that I will be reunited with Johnia when I pass from this earth. My daughter will be as beautiful and vibrant as the sun in the sky, and I will share everything with her that has happened since she joined her Heavenly Father.

Johnia accepted an internship with Chief Deputy Attorney General on the Court of Appeals Elizabeth McClanahan and spent some time with her. Elizabeth McClanahan spoke at Johnia's funeral about many of her achievements and some things that Johnia wrote.

Elizabeth McClanahan
Judge, Court of Appeals of Virginia

From Emily Dickinson:
Hope is a thing with feathers that perches in the soul. And sings the tune without the words and never stops at all.
(Scripted from the eulogy)
"Johnia Hope never stopped at all that's for sure. From elementary school through college, the awards and achievements are countless. Junior Beta Club, National Beta Club, Good Citizenship Award, Great Behavior Award, All-Star Cheerleader, Dean's List, National Honor Society, and she was the recipient of an Academy Performance Scholarship and Magna Cum Laude.

"In her life story, written in junior high school, she wrote, 'I try to do the best at everything I do, but most of all, I try to have fun!'

"Knowing Johnia's passion and love for a job well done, fun, and children, I have spent much of this week reading children's books that remind me of Johnia and all her qualities.

"Johnia was much like the very busy spider, diligently spinning her web and preparing for Miss Spider's tea party to share with all her friends. And share she did!

"Dr. Seuss, in The Lorax, said, 'Unless someone like you cares a whole awful lot, nothing is going to get better - it's not.'

"Johnia was the epitome of carrying a whole awful lot. She devoted herself to loving, sharing, and caring. From children to seniors, from the mentally ill to the physically challenged, I saw this first-hand, as she loved and energized my children and my mother this summer. She didn't hesitate to give me a few parenting lessons, as well

"Johnia gave all her time unconditionally and unselfishly. In the fift h grade, she wrote this poem about her time

Time is what you make of it.
All my time given to others. A waste? No.
All that time. I really like sharing it.

"*Johnia was smart and highly motivated, but most of all, kind, hopeful, and caring. And her infectious smile lit the world.*

"*In Charlotte's Web, Wilbur described his friend Charlotte after her death. He said she was 'in a class by herself,' and Johnia was most certainly in a class by herself.*

"*No one could walk into a room and light it up like Johnia. In fact, Johnia actually never walked into a room. She effervescently bounced into every room.*

"*I have known Johnia since she was four years old, and this summer had the special privilege and joy of having her intern in my office for about two months. The internship was unpaid for school credit. So, Johnia told me she would like to also work for me for pay in some other capacities at night and on weekends. That very busy spider was showing up again*

"*With confidence, she quickly listed for me all the roles that she could perform: chauffeur, swim instructor, valet, catering, cook, party planner, and most importantly, babysitter. She then concluded with an emphatic, 'I will not clean.'*

"*That statement told me Johnia was wise beyond her years! Her wisdom is shown in another fifth-grade poem she wrote entitled Lessons.*

Everything happens for a reason.
Each reason is a different lesson.
Each lesson has a special purpose.
Why is it that the most important lessons are the lessons no one ever learns?
One lesson that Max Lucado teaches in his children's book called Just In Case You Wonder is this.
And God wants me to make sure that you know about Heaven.
It's a wonderful place.

"But how do we make some sense out of this tragic taking of Johnia at such a young age? I look to the words of an old bluegrass hymn for comfort.

God's angels are gathering flowers for the Master's bouquet.
Beautiful flowers that will never fade.
Gathered by angels and carried away,
forever to bloom in the Master's bouquet.

—The Gathering Flowers for the Master's Boquet, **The Stanley Brothers**

"Johnna will forever bloom in our hearts, in the children she touched, and in Heaven."

Amber Kinsor, East Tennessee State University Professor (as transcribed from Johnia's Celebration of Life Ceremony)

Johnia Berry's spirit was a gift to my family. My children and I had the privilege of receiving this gift two years ago when I saw a sign she had posted at the East Tennessee Child Study Center—where she was working—advertising childcare.

The phone call I made to her was a significant moment for our family, because it expanded our sacred circle to include a woman who would devote herself to our family, nourishing my children tenderly and loving us all with the most genuine and unwavering affection, and she took her role in our family very seriously.

My husband and I called her our family assistant.

She saw herself as a sister to my six-year-old son and twelve-year-old daughter. And she treated them with great passion.

Worried that they would be hungry after school when she picked them up and took them to karate classes, she would stop and get them french fries to share. Chelsea told me this morning that she always took them for an after-school snack. (She was always trying to show me up!)

She took Chelsea shopping for dresses for her school dance-the kind of dresses as many of you would guess-that had more pink and flowers in them than most could stand.

Chelsea and I wore pink for her today.

She always made an extra trip to our house nearly every holiday to bring Isaac and Chelsea something celebratory—an Easter basket with toys that she had picked out for each of them, a trick-or-treat pumpkin filled with candy, or a Valentine's Day gift, or a birthday gift, or Christmas cards for each of them, and homemade holiday treats.

She helped Chelsea put her campaign for student council president together, putting together little bags of candy for her to hand out to coerce the children to vote for her. Johnia encouraged signs that said: Chelsea for president. It worked. They voted for her.

She would call me up and ask if she could take them to the movies or ice skating or swimming on her days off. Jason told me she called him and asked if he had any cool ideas to do with Isaac.

Her greatest gift to me is that she was kind and loving to my babies. Generous and tender-hearted in her care for them. When I was working late teaching until ten o'clock at night, I never gave thought to the well-being of my children, because they were in her loving hands.

Now, to the dismay of our current future family assistant, I am sure that she set the standards by which they all are measured.

They have heard—and will hear—too many times to suit them, I suspect:

> *"Well, Johnia always..."*
> *"Well, what I liked that Johnia did was..."*
> *"Johnia this" and "Johnia that."*

Every day she worked, she'd call me in the morning to see if there were any changes in the plans or anything else special that she needed to know. Now, two years later, she was still doing that. You see Johnia had a rhythm to her life, and I greatly admired it.

She spent two or three days a week for about two years with my children, she was an important part of our lives. We would've been lost without her.

I asked my son Isaac what he wanted me to say about her today, and he said, "She was really nice. She took me to get ice cream, and she had a good heart!"

My daughter Chelsea said, "I don't think she ever got mad at us. If she had no money, she always managed to give us gifts, and she was always in a happy mood. She made us feel good on sad days."

My husband, Patrick, is also a professor at ETSU, and he had Johnia in a class. He said she was in class every day over the summer at nine o'clock in the morning. Never late. She made A's on every assignment—except for one—and she made a B+, so the next day she brought in extra credit stuff. Because her standard was A, not B. Not even a high B. He said her work ethic was unassailable. He said she was always on time every day and pretty much did better in her work than everyone else in the room. He said to me in the car a couple of days ago that she was like a Ginger

Rogers joke. What makes Ginger Rogers better than Fred Astaire is that she does everything that Fred Astaire does—only backward and in high heels!

And Johnia managed to look better than everyone else somehow.

One of the things I like best about Johnia was that she was a no-nonsense, straight shooter. When she and I first talked about her working for us, she told me this is how much I make, this is how much I want to work, and I want to work at least two hours any day I work to make it worth my time.

And I thought, now this is a woman I can work with—somebody who knows what she wants and feels quite comfortable making that clear to other people.

As a professor, I've come in contact with a great many students over the last decade and a half. Johnia has put herself—chose to put herself—into the very small group of students who live life with a very strong internal locus of control. These are people who assume, I am the master of my life, if I want something I'll go get it. If I don't like a component in my life, I will change it! If there is a component missing from my life, I will create it myself!

I can only hope my children live their lives this way. And I think Johnia's example will help them do that.

I think, in our culture, it's especially difficult for women to live this way. Because they're taught to put others' needs first so much so that they never get to their own needs. I think my mother lives this way. But Johnia saw ways, found ways, and created ways, to grab from this life what she needed from it. And to do that without an apology.

If she needed money, she worked for it. Two or three jobs at a time if she needed to. And I never heard her talk about being put out by this. Ever. If she wanted an A, she did whatever it took to get it. If she wanted to do law school, she did whatever it took to get there. If she wanted something else, she just went and seized another opportunity. And she still managed, better than I could've, to care for others that mattered in her life along the way. There was a rhythm and tenacity to her way of life and to her way of living in this world that was nothing short of inspirational.

I would like to close with a piece that a friend of mine shared with me yesterday. It's a living eulogy that is typical of Johnia's life and our celebration of it today. It's written by Mary Anne Radmacher and it reads:

"She danced, she sang, she took, she gave, she served, she loved, she created, she descended, she enlivened, she saw, she grew, she sweat, she changed, she learned, she laughed, she shed her skin, she walked through walls, she lived with integrity."

Amber Kinser's words touched my heart.

So many people knew and loved Johnia, and they were shocked when she was murdered. How could my daughter—someone so pure and good—be taken from the world in such a violent way?

I can only trust God's plan.

Children from the Tri-State Baptist Children's Home sang at Johnia's funeral. "Jesus Loves Me" rang through the room.

Even in death, Johnia was beautiful. She wore a purple pantsuit and a purple scarf. I tried to pull the scarf away from her face, but I was told it had to be there to cover a very prominent stab wound.

The funeral and interment were on the same day. After the service, everyone left the ceremony.

My husband and I said our last goodbyes to our precious daughter. Thankfully, they closed the casket after I left. I couldn't imagine watching someone close the lid over my baby.

We drove to the cemetery in the rain, and it seemed like the angels released a torrent of tears over us. It was the same as the morning Johnia died.

Johnia was buried in a private cemetery. Her pallbearers were Jeremy Baker, Josey Baker, Robbie Hodge, Mark Young, James Rudolph, and Collin Jones. Stephen Morgan and a number of others were honorary pallbearers.

Joan's sister, Patti Baker, and her son, Josey

Years later, Josey Baker, my sister's son, passed away in a tragic accident. He was buried at the same cemetery. It saddens me that my sister lost a child, too.

Much like Johnia, Josey had everything going for him. He had a great family, and he was so happy.

I walked out of the cemetery in tears. Even though the outpouring of memories and emotions was a beautiful tribute to my daughter's life, it was a terribly painful day. My heart was completely broken, and a wound that deep never goes away.

On August 25, 2005, we held a candlelight memorial for Johnia. We gathered on the courthouse lawn in Abingdon, Virginia. I spoke, but it was hard to find words. I'm sure everyone knew how I felt, though.

We held another memorial on August 26, 2005, at the World's Fair Park in Knoxville, Tennessee.

We decided to hold the memorials in two locations for a number of reasons. Family and friends were in both areas. I had a business in Abingdon for eighteen years, and Johnia had been granted an apprenticeship under a former Justice of the Supreme Court of Virginia and had traveled with her.

The Knoxville detectives were at our daughter's funeral and participated in the memorial service. There had been no progress in Johnia's case, so it was important to keep her death in the public's mind.

It was hard, but the memorial was beautiful. At the end of the service, my grandchildren, Camryn and Cassidy Burke, came forward and sang the "Happy Birthday" song for Johnia, and mine weren't the only tears that fell for Johnia.

The friends and family of Johnia set up the Johnia Hope Berry Scholarship in Psychology fund. The scholarship helps support students who wish to pursue a career in child psychology. If you wish to donate to the fund, please address your envelope in care of the Johnia Hope Berry Memorial Scholarship, ETSU University Advancement, and send it to PO Box 70721, Johnson City, TN 37614.

Johnia's scholarship is offered at the College of Arts and Sciences at East Tennessee State University. I had a chance to visit the department in 2022, and I was received warmly. I'm glad the scholarship is still distributed to the young people who need it.

The celebration of my daughter's life wouldn't be complete without mentioning that she was an organ donor. Johnia had discussed with her dad several years before her murder that she wanted to be an organ donor.

Because she made the selfless decision to become a donor, others were granted more time. It takes a very special person to step outside selfish considerations and appreciate the needs of others.

Johnia always thought about other people. Even after her death, she continues to support others.

Even though I wish she could have stayed with us, I am thankful for the extension of life she granted the recipients. I can't express the deepest admiration I have for my sweet daughter and the everlasting love that lives on in my heart forever.

My daughter is buried in a private family cemetery along with my sister's son, Josey. Her father and I will be buried on either side of her. The tombstone shows all three of our names, but only one has a date of death. We placed a small picture of Johnia on her twenty-first birthday on the tombstone above her name.

Johnia penned a prayer, and I found it in a drawer after her death. I printed the prayer with a picture of her and made thank-you cards. Her beautiful words convey the thoughts I could echo to God, but I could never write them as eloquently.

Tombstone at Baker-Denton Cemetery

Prayer by:

Johnia Berry

I come to You, my Father, with my tears.

My tears of sin that I must beg forgiveness of.

My tears of pain that I must beg for relief of.

My tears of joy that I must beg for more of.

All my tears I bring to You, my Heavenly Father.

Each tear different and each with a small request.

I come to You because I know that You will listen.

I come to You, Father, with all my tears.

Johnia Berry (1983-2004)

I'm so glad there are no tears in heaven...

Above: Johnia's prayer in her handwriting.

It was found after her murder.

ETSU Graduation

On December 18, 2004, Mike and I attended the commencement ceremony at East Tennessee State University. Before Johnia was murdered, we thought we were going to watch our happy, confident daughter stride across the stage and receive her diploma, but we accepted it in her place.

The night before her death, we'd asked Johnia if she tried on her cap and gown.

The commencement was held on a sunny day, and it was beautiful. A ninety-nine-year-old graduate told the students about her days on campus and compared their experiences. She marveled at the freedoms they had compared to when she took classes at ETSU.

A group of students sang, and then the graduating class was asked to applaud their parents. It was hard not to cry.

Paul Stanton, the university's president, led a moment of silence for Johnia. He talked about how many lives she'd touched, and my heart broke.

Johnia should have been there to have received her Bachelor of Science degree and proudly relay her 3.78 grade-point average, but there we were, standing in line in her place. I wished I was watching her take her diploma, but I walked across the stage with her honor society medal in my hand as Mike accepted our daughter's diploma and magna cum laude ribbon. The cheers were a little louder when we accepted her diploma, but I hardly heard them as I climbed off stage.

I kept thinking it wasn't supposed to be this way. She was so excited about her college graduation. She would have thrown her cap in the air and cheered with her other classmates.

We stayed until the end. It was hard, but I did it for Johnia.

(from right) Dr. Paul E. Stanton and Johnia's parents, Joan and Mike Berry

We met so many of her friends. People who had classes with her approached us and offered their condolences.

We had planned to spend time with Johnia after her graduation and share Christmas with her, but there would be no Christmas for us. I couldn't look at the holiday the same ever again.

Imagine your hopes and dreams for your child or other treasured family member. You may want to see them graduate, get married, and have children. Johnia was going to do all those things. By no fault of her own, my daughter died without realizing her dreams, and my heart breaks every day for her loss and the accomplishments she'll never realize.

The Search for Johnia's Killer

Television, Radio, Billboard Spots, Conversation Board

We advertised the reward for the capture of Johnia's murderer on a billboard at the intersection of Interstate 40 and Cedar Bluff Road in Knoxville, Tennessee.

We gathered our own money, and friends and family helped us put together more funds for a reward. In February 2005, a ten-thousand-dollar reward was posted by the Knox County Sheriff's Office for information leading to the arrest and conviction of a suspect in my daughter's death.

The Carole Sund/Carrington Memorial Reward Foundation offered half of the reward, and an anonymous source posted part of it. The Carole Sund/Carrington Memorial Fund was established in honor of three women who were found murdered near Yosemite National Park in 1999. Our family was so grateful for the money offered by the organization and the anonymous source.

The Knox County Sherriff's Office received an abundance of calls when the reward was televised, but most of the information was duplicated from what they'd already gathered before the reward was mentioned. The sheriff's office received thirty or forty calls, but no new information surfaced.

We told the sheriff we were increasing the reward money and we'd like his approval, but he didn't think increasing the reward was necessary. We scheduled an interview and drove to the Tri-Cities. On the way there, I was contacted by a friend from Knoxville who informed me that the sheriff was going to make an announcement in regard to my daughter's case.

"I don't know what it could be," I said.

Sheriff Tim Hutchison addressed news cameras and announced the reward only hours before we were scheduled to talk about it to the media. He succeeded in getting ahead of us. He knew we were going to announce an addition to the reward, and he didn't want to look bad.

I was disappointed in the sheriff's reaction when Mike and I told him about the increase in the reward. I was thankful, though, that he did the right thing by asking for any information that would lead to an arrest and conviction in Johnia's murder.

Within a year, the reward increased to $37,000, and before the end of 2005, Governor Phil Bredesen announced the State of Tennessee would offer $2500 to the person who gave information leading to the arrest and conviction of a suspect, and Channel 8 in Knoxville added $5,000. Friends and family gave more money until the reward was $70,000 at the beginning of 2006.

In Atlanta, Georgia, we stood outside a book signing for hours to tell Johnia's story to Nancy Grace, and she agreed to have us on her show. The show aired on November 25, 2005, and the transcript can be found online.

She started her interviews with Tim Hutchison of the Knox County Sherriff's Office. They discussed the evidence that had been released to the public and the need to expand the DNA database to include everyone in the state who had been convicted of a violent crime, even if it was later reduced to a misdemeanor. She moved on to talk to Mike and me, and she spoke to a clinical psychologist. We appealed to the public to help us, and the actual 911 call was played.

I reached out to America's Most Wanted and asked if they could film a story on Johnia's case. They said they could do a case but would need the sheriff's approval. The sheriff would not grant his approval.

Would more national exposure have helped Johnia's case? I guess we'll never know.

Our family was angered by the decision. Arrests were not forthcoming, so more national exposure could have led them to the killer sooner.

After the sheriff turned down help from America's Most Wanted, he made the statement that it would create too many false leads. He expressed that his department had spent more money on Johnia's case than any other case.

I rightfully wondered, *How is Johnia's case going to be solved without leads?*

It shouldn't have been about the money! It should have involved finding the person that murdered Johnia and getting that person off the streets before that individual committed any more violent crimes!

After the sheriff refused help from America's Most Wanted, I traveled to Nashville, Tennessee, to visit with the Director of the Tennessee Bureau of Investigation, Mark Gwyn. He was the TBI's first Black director, and he served fourteen years, the longest term a TBI director has served.

Of course, he already knew about Johnia's case. I explained my fears and concerns that Johnia's case would turn into a cold case. I asked if the TBI could help or if they would be willing to look at Johnia's case.

Director Gwyn was ready to help us, but he needed to be invited by the Knoxville Sheriff's Department to contribute to the investigation. The TBI assisted small rural counties, and Knoxville was considered a city. Director Gwyn told me that he would send in his best investigators, but they had to have the sheriff's invitation.

I made an appointment with Sheriff Hutchison. Mike and I traveled to Knoxville to ask if he would allow the TBI to look at Johnia's case.

We weren't asking for the TBI to take the case over. We only wanted them to look at the evidence. Others may see things differently, and what would it hurt to have a new set of eyes look at Johnia's case?

Again, he refused! Sheriff Hutchison informed me they did not need any help in Johnia's case.

I couldn't believe what I had heard! Tears of despair ran down my face!

I recall saying to him, "Letting the TBI look at the case would not cost any revenue to Knox County."

He was unmovable.

Where Can You See Johnia's Story?

Montel Williams
Nancy Grace (3 times)
Paula Zahn (2 times)
Forensic files
   City Confidential "Trail of Terror" (Aired December 16, 2021)
   Oxygen Sleeping with Death "Left for Dead" (November 6, 2022)

I hoped telling Johnia's story would bring attention to how important DNA laws are to have in every state. Also, I wanted to make everyone aware that a tragedy could happen to anyone.
My husband and I never thought it would happen to our daughter.

Community Meeting
Friday, January 19
at Cokesbury Center
9915 Kingston Pike, Knoxville
6pm

Johnia Hope Berry

On Friday, January 19, 2007, Dena Hysmith helped me organize a community meeting. She invited the Knox County Sheriff's Department, District Attorney Randy Nichols, and Tennessee House Representative Stacey Campfield. Though they responded to the request, none of them came to the event; however, over fifty citizens filled the seats as I shared the most recent developments in Johnia's case.

I was determined to keep Johnia's case in the hearts and minds of Knoxville citizens, and the meeting was established to update everyone about the case and receive support from the community to continue our search for Johnia's killer.

A message board was formed to keep the conversation about Johnia's death alive. Johnia's friends, family, and people who were affected when they heard the news of her death posted comments regularly. I think Johnia would have been glad people were bonding, and friends were reconnecting over the messages. She may have been disappointed over the disagreements over the level of importance certain people played in her life, but Johnia would have been happy that her brother, Kelly, posted his feelings and memories of her on the message board.

(The following was written by Johnia's brother, Kelly. She called him Eddie, as his middle name is Edward.)

From, Eddie
(Shared with permission from Kelly Burke)

I got the call around 5:40 AM on December 6, 2004. It wasn't my work cell phone ringing, so I knew it had to be close to me. Someone who desperately needed to talk.

Who else would call my house line at this hour?

I groped around for the phone, picked it up, and leaned over the bed.

"Hello?"

The voice on the other end was instantly recognizable. *How couldn't it be?* I'd heard it for thirty-one years of my life. It was Joan, my mom. I quickly recognized that something was terribly wrong. There was something in her voice. Someone had been hurt.

My mother was sobbing and yelling. "Oh my god! My baby! I have to get to my baby! Hurry! I have to get to my baby!"

It was clear to me that she was in the car on her way somewhere. The person she was yelling at wasn't me—it was surely Mike, my stepfather. I wasn't certain that she knew I was on the line at that second.

"Mom, Mom! What's going on? What's happened? Mom?"

I'm not an early riser. Anyone who knows me can attest to that. Stirring at any hour before eight seems out of the ordinary for me, but there was something in my mother's voice that instantly shook me from my slumber.

I was wide-eyed, awake, and on my feet, staring into the darkness of my room.

"Mom! Talk to me! What's going on?"

"Oh my god, hurry! I have to get to my baby! She's all alone! All alone!"

"Mom! What's happened?"

For some reason, I thought of the family dog, Sugar. I don't know why, but the image of the thirteen-year-old terrier came to mind. She had come to live with us as a puppy. She was a gift for my sister, Johnia. The old dog had suffered a few health problems over the last few months. This was surely what my mom was calling about. *What in the world else could be wrong?*

"Mom?"

"Kelly, Kelly! I'm sorry! I'm sorry to call you like this!

"Someone broke into Johnia's apartment! She's been stabbed! It's not good! It's not good!"

"Mom, no! What's happened? What's happened?"

"You have to get to the hospital! She's all alone! You have to get to the hospital!"

"Okay, okay! Where is she?"

My shoes were on. I was ready to go. Rachel, my girlfriend, was also up, clearly aware that something was horribly wrong. She was tying her shoes as I flipped on the light.

"Mom, is she okay? Is she all right?"

I tried my best to be calm. Maybe only to calm her if I could.

"It's not good, Kelly. I'm sorry."

"Mom, is she okay?"

"They called us! They called us!"

She stopped for a second and got her breath again.

"He said we need to come identify the body."

My sister, Johnia, had moved to Knoxville six weeks prior to the phone call. On the morning of December sixth, her objective was to begin class at UT in pursuit of a master's degree, but in the meantime, she had accepted a position at Penninsula Hospital, where she worked in the adolescent wing. And with the Christmas season upon us, she had taken a part-time job with Zales in West Town Mall to earn some extra money to buy gifts.

She had also just finished her coursework at East Tennessee State University, where she was to walk the stage with a 3.78 GPA. December eighteenth was the day she was supposed to accept this incredible achievement.

So, with twelve short days to go to ETSU's graduation, I sped down Pellissippi Parkway in the pouring rain toward UT Hospital. Rachel had asked if I wanted to pray and ask God to save my sister. I hadn't told her what my mom said about identifying the body. There was no time.

Mostly, I was concentrating on a road full of standing water. At the speed I was traveling, that should have been my only concern, but my goal was to get to the hospital to be with my sister, just like my mom had asked.

It was 6:20 AM when I pulled into the parking lot in front of UT Hospital. I climbed out of my car and checked my watch. (My mom was still a few hours away if she was coming from Atlanta.) Rachel followed me through the automatic doors leading to the ER.

"My name is Kelly Burke, and I'm here about the stabbing in West Knoxville. I'm here for my sister."

The reaction on the receptionist's face went blank. "And you're the brother?'

"Yes, yes, that's right. Where's my sister?"

"One moment, please."

The receptionist stood and walked away. A few officers were standing near the door of a small office just a few feet away, and they looked at the receptionist as she approached them.

After a couple of moments, one of the officers walked my way.

"Sir? Could you follow me?"

I could. But I really don't want to.

"What happened? I want to know where she is. I want to know what happened."

A lady wearing a winter hat stepped toward me, held a Styrofoam cup of coffee low, and looked me in the face.

"I'm a detective, and I'd like to ask you a few questions."

"What happened? Where is my sister?"

"Sir, if you'll just follow me, I'll answer your questions."

The formality of filling out forms, and answering questions, seemed so surreal to me at the time, but there was nothing else to do. I listened to the questions, stared straight ahead, nodded, mumbled, and answered one or two.

"Could you please spell your sister's name?"

I did.

"Where did she live?"

I told her.

"Is my sister dead?" I asked.

"There's a young woman who passed away. Can you tell me if your sister had her belly button pierced?"

I looked at Rachel. My mind raced out of my head and into the wet, black clouds that hung over the hospital and fell back into my skull.

"Yes, yes. She had a small piercing in her belly button."

The detective nodded slightly. She scribbled something on the form in front of her.

"Sir, if you'll just step over here, someone will be right with you. We will need you to identify the deceased person if you can."

I felt like my soul drifted out of my body and tried to hide in the bushes outside of the ER. I followed it into the rain and pulled my cell phone from my pocket.

"Gran, I need Aunt Patti's number. What? No. Mom is okay. I just need Aunt Patti's cell phone number. I need to talk to her. No, Gran, Mom's okay. She's fine."

"Oh God, it's Johnia. Something happened to Johnia!" she said.

"Gran, I need Aunt Patti's phone number."

"Kelly, please," my grandmother pleaded. "Don't lie to me. Something's happened to Johnia, hasn't it? Something's happened."

There's a time in every family's history when you try to protect someone if there's nothing that person can do. Why worry them about something so far away, something so far out of their control? Less is more, I guess. This wasn't a time for lies.

"Yes, Gran. Johnia's dead." Even without final confirmation, I knew that to be the truth. I lowered the cell to my side as my Gran screamed into the phone.

My brother, Tim, pulled into a parking spot, climbed out of his truck, and looked at me. I shut the phone and shoved it into my back pocket. We approached each other slowly.

"Is she...? Dead?"

"Yeah, Tim. I'm pretty sure she is."

And for the first time in years that I can remember, my brother and I embraced.

The next hour or so passed, and my mother's sister, Aunt Patti, pulled in, and I repeated the same words I had to my brother and grandmother. Aunt Patti had driven down from Bristol, Tennessee, with my Uncle Jerry, my cousin, and her husband.

Tim stepped away from the group and called his wife, Kristie, to tell her the news.

"Johnia was stabbed to death this morning," he said into the phone. "No, don't cry. Don't cry. You'll scare the girls."

My brother is the father of three incredible, beautiful little girls—who, by the way, resemble lovely fairies and take after my sister, naturally.

I stood a few feet away from him, staring toward the entrance to the ER, wondering when my mom would pull in. Hopefully, it would be a few more minutes.

Hopefully.

And as if someone was listening to my wishes, the man with a clipboard stepped into the lobby, approached the family, and cleared his throat.

"Are you the brothers?"

"Yes, we're the brothers," I confirmed.

"Hello, sir. If you'll just step over here."

Tim and I followed.

"I need to show you a photograph. See if this is your sister."

I looked at Tim. He looked at me. We braced ourselves.

"Now, I want you fellows to know that this is not like a funeral picture. We've cleaned up the victim the best we could, but this isn't going to be easy. There is some blood. There is some blood."

There was something in the way he said "victim."

I stared down at the clipboard as the man flipped the front page back, revealing the printout below. As I had so desperately feared, I gazed down at the very last photograph ever taken of my sister. Her beautiful blonde hair was matted in blood.

The man tilted the clipboard back a bit, and the picture slid into view of the rest of the family.

"Please, please!"

I grabbed the clipboard and flipped the front page back to hide my sister's face.

"Sorry, sir. Sorry."

He paused and fumbled for a pen. "Is this your sister?"

"Yes."

"Okay, if you'll just sign here. Just sign right here."

I took the pen from the man's hand and pressed it hard into the paper. I scratched my name the best I could and gave it back to him.

Was this what the process was like for every family who faced this?

It was as cold and empty as signing for delivery. It's not like in the movies, where they're ushered into a room with a body under a sheet. There was only a colored picture of my sister's lifeless face.

"I'm sorry, sir. I'm really sorry."

I staggered through the sliding doors into the rain and plodded along the front drive leading into the ER. Not even a minute passed before my mom's car pulled in.

It was about two hundred yards from the ER entrance. Mike stopped the car, and my mom stepped out into the rain. Her face was ashen white and wet with tears.

"What is it? What's happened?"

"She's gone, Mom. She's gone."

Her tears flowed harder.

"I know. I know."

She paused for a moment, grabbed my shoulders, and squeezed hard. "Did they hurt her face? Did they hurt my baby's face?"

She trembled and stared into my eyes, waiting for an answer.

They—the killer—did more than hurt my sister's face. They stripped the family—and the world—of one more beautiful person, who wanted nothing more than to live a happy life. And as we all sat around the ER, waiting for the final word on when my sister's body would be sent to Bristol, my hometown.

I remember watching my mom huddle on the curb, sobbing into her hands.

"I just want to die. I just want to die now."

Three days later, after hiding out in an empty room of the funeral home on the night of my sister's wake, I finally stepped out to join the rest of the family to receive friends. I remember keeping my eyes away from the open casket that held Johnia's body. I couldn't look. This couldn't be real.

Scores of people turned out to pay their final respects to my fallen sister. It wasn't clear to me just how many people's lives she had touched in her short stay on this earth, but that night, it was more than obvious. Hours passed as my family and I shook hands and hugged people, some of whom we'd never met before.

"I just wanted you to know how much your sister meant to me," a stranger told me. "She was truly one of a kind. I just can't believe something like this has to happen to someone like her."

Sentiments like that were offered the rest of the night. A young man even told me that Johnia had stopped him from committing suicide. His voice shook as he recounted how she had talked him out of killing himself. I thanked him for telling me, and he walked away to have a last look at the person who saved his life, hers now taken.

My mom and Mike stood in front of the casket and personally thanked hundreds of people who had waited in line to offer their condolences.

"She looks beautiful," I would overhear someone say to my mother. "So peaceful and so beautiful. And they would step over to the casket to stare down at Johnia, standing there for a few moments beside my mom, tears silently falling down their faces, hands locked together, before disappearing into the crowd of people still gathered in the hallway.

My grandfather is a tough man—one of the toughest I've ever known. He rarely showed emotion, but as the crowd thinned, I glimpsed him across the room. He stared at my sister, and tears were streaming down his face. It seemed like forever before he turned and walked away.

Once I finally mustered up the strength, I approached the pink casket and looked down at Johnia's body lying inside. Her golden hair framed her face, and there was a scarf around her neck. Her engagement ring was on her pinky finger. Jason, her fiancé, had put it there since her ring finger was too swollen. There were a number of pictures on her chest, put there by friends. Someone had written a letter and had tucked it into one of her coat pockets. I gently took her right hand and slid a flower carefully beneath it. And, for the longest time, I cried for Johnia.

Nine days later, we went to ETSU's graduation ceremony. My family and I traveled to Johnson City for the occasion. Hundreds of joyous students gathered in the Mini Dome to accept their degrees, and I watched from the stands as Mom and Mike took a seat up front among the excited graduates. As they were named, another student accepted their degree.

I felt a huge knot in my stomach as my mom approached the stage with Mike at her side. Even from a distance, I could see the pain on her face as she and Mike made the walk my sister should have made. Johnia's name was called out, there was a moment of silence, and my mom accepted my sister's degree.

Christmas 2004 was even more painful. The gifts Johnia had bought with the money from her second job were found neatly placed on the floor of her apartment. She never had a chance to wrap them or sign the Winnie the Pooh cards found with the rest of the gifts.

On Christmas Eve, my mom handed out the presents my sister had purchased for my three nieces. The rest of us received Winnie the Pooh cards—all unsigned.

Ten surreal months have crawled by since the murder of my sister. The deepest grief and pain have followed me nearly every minute of the day.

How couldn't it?

But I find rage and fury have managed to find equal billing. I sometimes daydream of running across the killer myself—with no one else around.

I've shed countless tears for my sister. Like anyone who experiences the tragic loss of a loved one, I've struggled to find reasonable ways to cope.

Johnia touched many lives and could have touched many, many more. But, as life often shows us, other people in the world are the polar opposite of Johnia—people who are motivated by darker things.

More than ten months have passed since someone murdered my sister on that rainy December morning. Some days are harder to get through than others, but they're never easy.

I often think of Johnia and what she must have felt during her final moments. *Was she crying as she died? Was she in pain? Was she calling out for her mom? For Mike, her dad? God?*

And then I think about her killer. That person stabbed my sister while I slept peacefully only a few miles away.

He continues to breathe and enjoy life, unlike Johnia.

Did he think he would get away with taking her life? So far, he has.

The detectives from Knox County Sheriff's Office have been working tirelessly on the case since day one. For this, my family and I thank them. But some cases are harder to solve than others. This seems to be one of those cases.

Who would kill my sister and why? One thing I know for sure is that if this happened to me, Johnia would—at this very moment—be doing everything in her power to help find my killer. I vow to do no less.

But I must sadly accept my sister's fate. Perhaps I will see her again. But one thing I will never accept is the notion that the worthless human who killed my sister will get away with his crime.

Like all of us, his time will come. I only pray that the time is soon.

The Manhunt for Johnia's Killer Continues

Assistant Chief Deputy Keith Lyons

Assistant Chief Deputy Lynn Keith Lyons, with the Knoxville Sheriff's Office, spearheaded Johnia's murder investigation. Later, I found out he and other investigators had attended Johnia's funeral.

After the funeral, Mike and I went to the Knoxville Sheriff's Department. On that day, we met Chief Lyons.

I called him every day and visited Knoxville frequently, so we were soon on a first-name basis. On one of the visits my husband and I made to Knoxville, we had lunch with Keith and Detective Amy Lynn Delgado. That day, Mike and I discovered the State of Tennessee did not take DNA from felons.

Immediately I declared, "That needs to be changed!"

When I visited Keith's office, I saw dozens of cardboard boxes and a filing cabinet. Each box was part of Johnia's case. On the wall, a sizeable laminated diagram of Johnia's apartment was visible, a blueprint with many marks tracing a path. He was dedicated to finding Johnia's murderer.

Groups of eight to twelve people followed leads on Johnia's murder under his command. Mostly though, Detectives Delgado and Hall handled the investigation.

On May 9, 2006, I was working in Atlanta and received a call from my son, Kelly. Keith had been killed in an automobile accident. A vehicle had crossed the center line and struck his police-issued SUV. Keith and the other driver died before they made it to the hospital.

What a sad day! Keith had been with the police department for eighteen years and was only forty-two years old.

I was devastated. I could not believe he was dead.

I trusted Keith. He was a kindhearted, caring man, and it made me anxious that he would not be at the Knox County Sheriff's Office. Most of all, I felt for his family. They had to endure the pain of such a loss. He had only been in the middle of his life!

Mike and I attended his funeral a few days later. He was such a good man, and I am thankful for the attention he gave to my daughter's murder case.

Johnia Berry Act

Mike and I were glad to find out the killer left DNA at the scene of the crime, but we had no idea that the National Data Base lacked critical information to help solve crimes. That's when we worked to make a change to the laws in Tennessee.

We know nothing can ever bring Johnia back. No law can ever change what happened to her. In the end, Johnia is gone, and our hearts are forever broken. No words can express our pain.

In regard to the publicity, we were lucky. The attention helped pull Johnia's investigation into the light and kept it from becoming a cold case. Johnia's murder investigation was considered high-profile and gained significant media attention. But two and half years into the investigation, 400 DNA samples had been reviewed and over 1,000 individuals had been interviewed, but Johnia had received no justice.

My husband and I worked hard to get The Johnia Berry Act 2007 passed. There were many roads to navigate in the six months from the proposal until it was instituted. The Senate and the House of Representatives supported our cause and pushed through an act many Tennesseans already thought was included in our state laws.

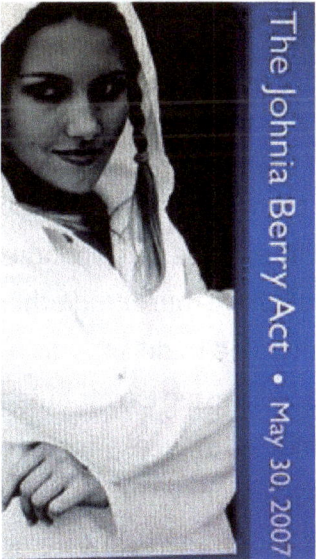

In 1990, fourteen states participated in a program called the Combined DNA Index System (CODIS). It enabled authorities to take DNA samples from suspects who were incarcerated, convicted of a felony, or facing charges. Even though it was released as a national endeavor, due to questions of constitutionality, ranging from illegal search and seizure to self-incrimination, Tennessee was not—originally—part of that program.

On May 9, 2007, the Johnia Berry Act 2007 was passed. The new law states that a person who is arrested for a violent felony must have a DNA sample taken and submitted to the Tennessee Bureau of Investigation.

Tennessee Minority Leader Jason Mumpower sponsored the bill. Governor Phil Bredesen signed the Johnia Berry Act 2007 into law.

Governor Phil Bredesen signs 'The Johnia Berry Act' into law. - May, 2007

The Johnia Berry Act of 2007 required all persons arrested for certain violent crimes to have a DNA sample taken. The Tennessee Bureau of Investigation (TBI) receives the DNA sample, and they can keep it on file if the suspect is convicted of the charges, but they have to destroy the specimen if the accused is expunged.

The Johnia Berry Act requires DNA to be taken from anyone arrested for first- or second-degree murder, aggravated kidnapping, aggravated arson, carjacking, aggravated assault, aggravated child abuse, robbery or aggravated robbery, sexual battery, sexual battery by an authority figure, or aggregated sexual battery, and rape, aggravated rape, or rape of a child. The act yielded results soon after it was enacted.

On September 24, 2007, a DNA match led to the arrest of a man for the murder of our daughter. He was allowed to walk around free for thirty-four months after viciously murdering our precious Johnia. He committed more crimes and could have murdered other people during that time if he had been compelled to do so.

If Tennessee had instituted the DNA Felony Arrestee Law, Johnia's murderer would have been known in a matter of weeks instead of years. It would have also saved Tennessee money, not to mention our family the unbelievable pain of not knowing who murdered our only daughter.

In 2007, The Johnia Berry Act was passed. It took two years to get The Johnia Berry Act passed. Currently, only thirty-nine states have enacted the law. Eleven states, including Idaho and Nebraska, have yet to pass it.

It is my hope that sharing the story of Johnia's murder will bring awareness to the fact that DNA arrestee laws should be passed in all states. And my prayer is that another family will not have to endure the pain of losing a loved one.

(from left) Joan Berry and Jon Lundberg

Jon Lundberg was a House Representative when the Johnia Berry Act 2007 was passed. He was always so helpful and kind to my family, and I appreciated his help.

Sometime after the act was passed, he shared a sweet story about his son, Nelson, with me. Representative Lundberg had felt the heavy burden that sometimes weighs on people in the legislative branch of our country's government. He had toyed with the idea of quitting his political career.

Jon's nine-year-old son, Nelson, was spending the day at the Tennessee State Capitol building with his father on the day the Johnia Berry Act 2007 was passed. On the way home that evening, Nelson expressed his pride in his father's position. He felt his father's work was important, and Nelson encouraged him to keep doing it.

Jon Lundberg is now a state senator.

Manhunt and Capture

On a dark, dreary, rainy day on December 9, 2004, our only daughter was laid to rest in a private cemetery. On December 10, 2004, our journey with law enforcement started. Finding the person who murdered Johnia became my new goal in life. It consumed my every waking moment.

After meeting with detectives from the Knox County Sheriff's Department, we discovered three different types of DNA were found in the apartment. Johnia and Jason Aymami's DNA was identified, but an unknown DNA was uncovered.

Despite the DNA evidence, until 2007, the State of Tennessee did not take DNA upon arrest. DNA was only taken after a felony conviction, which meant if the accused pled down to a lesser charge, he or she may never have to give a DNA sample. Additionally, the killer may not have been to jail previously.

Mike and I started working with Tennessee legislators to get a law passed to collect DNA upon felony arrest. Lieutenant Governor Ron Ramsey, Representative Steve Godsey, Representative Jason Mumpower, Senator Jon Lundberg, and Representative Tim Burchett (now Congressman Tim Burchett), worked tirelessly to get this law in place. Tennessee was the eighth state to pass the DNA collection at felony arrest law. But even after this legislative milestone, we were still waiting for justice, and it had been twenty months since Johnia's murder with no suspect in custody.

Just after Johnia's death, my husband and I posted a $5,000 reward for any information about the man who murdered our daughter. Over time, however, it increased to $70,000 for information that led to the arrest and conviction of the person who murdered Johnia.

There were billboards, mobile billboards, local media, television, and newspaper advertisements. The website, Johniaberry.org, was created in hopes of spreading awareness about her murder and bringing her story into mainstream news.

Johnia's story was aired on CNN, Nancy Grace, and Paula Zahn. I was apprehensive her case would turn into a cold case, and I worked hard to keep her image in the media, letting folks know there was a murderer still walking freely on our streets.

The reward information was posted on the back of Food City trucks as they traveled up and down the interstate from Virginia to Georgia. On my days off work, I drove to Knoxville and the Tri-Cities and put fliers on doors in apartment complexes and parked cars. I walked around shopping centers and handed out fliers. I let the media know I was coming to ensure we had coverage.

I was so desperate for any shred of a lead that I tried everything. I went on the Montel Williams Show and asked Sylvia Brown questions. We scheduled a reading with Bobby Drinnon, but he was booked for a year. A nice lady gave her appointment to me so I could see him sooner.

The sheriff's department agreed to let us use a hairbrush and the detachable tail for Johnia's stuffed Eeyore, so we could receive a reading from Noreen Renier. A detective called her, and we received the transcript notes. Without knowledge of the case, she described an intense struggle and a word the killer repeated that started with the letter C.

Renier concentrated on the killer's appearance, particularly citing an overbite. Sadly, nothing she related brought us closer to finding Johnia's killer.

Just before her death, Johnia called Mike and asked him for directions to a movie theater. He didn't remember if she said she was going with anyone and was concerned that the possible friend may know something about her murder. A movie ticket was discovered, but the theater didn't have cameras.

We went to a hypnotist in Atlanta, Georgia, and Mike went under. I was allowed to sit quietly in the room, and I watched as my husband's face lost all color.

Mike remembered the experience, but he couldn't pinpoint additional information. I'm glad we went through the process, though. It was better to try to gain more information on our own than sit on our hands and wait.

My husband and I were in constant contact with the Knox County detectives, but there were no real leads for a couple of years. It took two years and ten months before an arrest was made.

Two years after Johnia's death, an anonymous caller phoned the hotline number. He said he recognized the sketch of the perpetrator. He stated that it looked like someone he knew: Taylor Olson.

Detectives were in Philadelphia, Pennsylvania, at a "think tank" for officers in special crimes units when Detectives Hall and Delgado received the tip about Taylor Olson. They looked up his background and criminal history before driving back to Tennessee to interview him.

In 2005, Taylor Olson was charged with credit card theft and forgery, but it wasn't enough to require a DNA sample under the current Tennessee law. Olson was a person of interest in Johnia's murder in 2007, but the investigators didn't have his sample to compare against the DNA found at Johnia's apartment.

In late July 2007, Olsen was arrested for a probation violation. Investigators found him at a residence where marijuana plants were growing. He ran and hid in a basement, where investigators were finally able to talk him into leaving with them.

Olson had an outstanding warrant in another jurisdiction, but before the investigators turned him over, they questioned him about Johnia. Olson denied knowing her or ever stepping foot into her apartment.

Without more to go on than a vague similarity to the composite sketch, the investigators collected a voluntary DNA sample from him. The officers carried kits with swabs in them while on duty. They had run hundreds of DNA samples, paying for some of them out of the department's funds.

After Olsen gave the sample, he was turned over to the other jurisdiction for processing. Olson was released from jail but was arrested again in August 2007 for burglary and theft.

When detectives interviewed him, they noticed scars on his hand and arm. He explained them away, saying he had received the one on his arm in military school and that he had punched a lightbulb, and it had cut his hand.

On September 24, 2007, a DNA match led to the arrest of Taylor Lee Olson for the murder of Johnia Berry. We were told the DNA match was a 6.8 billion to 1 match. Paired with his partial fingerprint on the knife, it seemed like Johnia's killer would finally be brought to justice.

Almost three years after he murdered Johnia, twenty-two-year-old Taylor Lee Olson was indicted for felony murder, first-degree murder, attempted first-degree murder, and attempted burglary. Other than some lesser crimes, Olson had no weighty criminal history. Up to that point, he was not required by law to provide a DNA sample to the investigators.

In the recordings of the interview, Olson asked the detectives if they were "joking" when they told him his DNA matched the sample. They let him go back to a cell, but they called him back two days later and questioned him again. He'd had plenty of time to think about his situation.

Olson broke down and confessed. He said, "It was like a fight," and "I freaked out."

In the recording, Detective Hall touched Olson's arm. He lied about where and how he had gotten the scar.

Olson confessed to trying doors on the backside of Brendon Apartments until he found an unlocked door. Using the light from his cell phone, he looked for keys to a car in the kitchen and living room, but he couldn't locate them.

"I needed a car," he said.

Jason's bedroom door was on the right-hand side of the hallway. His door was closed but his television was on. Johnia left her bedroom door cracked, so Olson slipped in, looking for keys with a fob. He hoped to locate a car more easily with the locator on the fob.

Olson stated that Johnia woke up and spoke to him. "Relax" or "Chill" was his response.

How many women have been told the same thing before they were violated or killed? We've all heard the stories, and Johnia had, too. She was scared, and she had no idea who was in her room, his intentions, or if he was carrying a weapon.

After all, Olson didn't flee when she spoke. If he was only there for her car keys, he could have stated his intentions. He could have run away. It was clear from his statement that she gave him the chance. She would have chosen to hand over her car keys instead of dying, but she didn't know he was there for them.

Olson chose to stab Johnia. She fought back fiercely, and that's evident from the crime scene. She struggled against him, but he was too enraged. He stabbed her until she was too weak from her wounds to fight back.

When reporters asked him why he killed Johnia, he said, "I'm sorry. I never meant for this to happen. It was an accident."

How do you *accidentally* stab someone over twenty times?

Even with the DNA evidence, some people argued that Noah Cox had killed our daughter. They cited the similarities to his features in the police sketch. However, the DNA match says it all. Taylor Lee Olson killed my daughter, Johnia Hope Berry. He stabbed her numerous times in the face, neck, hands, and chest as she tried to defend herself. He took my daughter from me, and it was finally time for him to see justice for his crimes.

Murderer

Taylor Lee Olson was born in Eugene, Oregon on April 3, 1985. If only he had stayed in Oregon! Maybe he could have met some good friends and lived a better life instead of breaking into apartments and attempting to steal car keys, an act that led to my daughter's murder.

Olson was allowed things Johnia couldn't have, like more time to live and a chance to say goodbye. My daughter wasn't given precious moments to write her final thoughts to us or send her love.

Olson escaped justice for almost three years after he stabbed my daughter to death. He saw sunrises and sunsets, had a girlfriend, got into more trouble, and sired a child.

When the police led him on what they call the "perp walk", he was bound in handcuffs. A reporter asked him why he did it.

Taylor Lee Olson

Olson tried to act like it was an accident, but the reporter cornered him. She told him how many times he'd stabbed Johnia.

Twenty-six times.

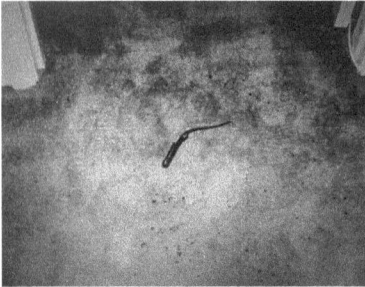

Photo of the knife at the crime scene

Courtesy of the Knox County Sheriff's Department

Olson admitted to authorities that he had been drinking and smoking marijuana with Noah Cox before they decided to steal a car. They were in the middle of burglarizing a car when an alarm went off. They had stolen CDs, a car stereo, and two hats, which they used to cover their heads from the rain. The owner of the items discovered Olson and Cox outside. They ran from the scene, and they started trying to open doors along the back of the building where my daughter lived, searching for an unlocked door.

What right did he have to be in the apartment? Why was he in her bedroom? Why didn't he just run away when she spoke?

Olson was selfish. He was there for what he wanted, and he wasn't leaving without car keys.

My daughter was strong and ready to defend herself. She fought him with everything she had in her.

Did she fight him over her car keys? No. I doubt she even knew why he was in her bedroom.

As a woman, I know what I would think if a man were in my room and told me to "chill out" instead of running away when I spoke. I would think he was there to hurt or kill me.

And he did hurt and kill her. Stabbing her and running away wasn't good enough for him. He stabbed my daughter over twenty-five times.

He wasn't done though.

As he backed out of her room, Jason Aymami open his door, and Olson attacked him, too. He didn't want there to be any witnesses to his crime. Otherwise, he would have run away instead of attacking Jason.

That's the reason I can't believe his crocodile tears. He could have run away. At any time, he could have made a decision that wouldn't have killed and traumatized someone. At any point, he could have stopped.

Taylor Olson *chose* to stab Johnia and Jason. He decided to end one life and destroy another.

What more can I say about the man who murdered my daughter?

This section is short and with good reason. My daughter's murderer doesn't deserve a significant part in her story. He only receives a few lines to show the monster who extinguished a radiant light. The world will recall Johnia's beautiful soul and her compassion, but he will only be remembered as a murderer.

I prepared to sit in a courtroom and finally have justice for Johnia. On March 24, 2008, though, I received a call that changed the direction of Johnia's case.

Facts About the Case and Suspects

Johnia was a young woman with lots of hopes and dreams. She was my daughter, and in a lot of ways, she was still a child to me. Even though she was responsible and made adult decisions, traces of her youth were around her.

Her childhood toy, Eeyore, was in Johnia's room when she was murdered. There was blood on Eeyore and the sheriff's department held onto it with her other things for evidence. Eeyore was returned to us eventually, but he had splatters of blood on him.

It's hard to think of my young daughter hugging that toy with a bright smile, and later, it was splattered with her blood as she fought for her life. It seems completely out of place. But, of course, my daughter should never have been murdered.

Johnia at a character
meet-and-greet with Eeyore at
Magic Kingdom in Disney World

Over 1,000 people were interviewed in the investigation of Johnia's murder. I waited, hoping each suspect would lead us closer to Johnia's killer.

Johnia and Jason's apartment was marked with crime scene tape for several weeks as detectives ripped up blood-splattered sections of carpet and took out pieces of the wall. An indention in the wall was made when Jason kicked his attacker away from him, and the detectives removed that part of the wall, too. They left no stone unturned.

Even though he'd been injured, Jason Aymami, Johnia's room-mate was originally a suspect. Rumors circulated that they were romantically entangled, but anyone who knew them quickly dismissed the idea. On the night of Johnia's murder, Jason may have forgotten to lock the back door after he took out the trash, but he didn't stab her multiple times.

Courtesy of Knox County Sheriff's Department

Blood was taken from the bedroom, front room, and outside the back door. It didn't match Johnia's or Jason's blood, so the sheriff's department tried to match it with samples from known assailants and members of her close family and friends.

Why did it take so long to get the DNA back? Well, the sheriff's department pulled DNA from seventy-four individuals and sent it to the Tennessee Bureau of Investigation (TBI) laboratory in Nashville, Tennessee. From there, it took two and a half months for the TBI and the Federal Bureau of Investigation (FBI) lab in Quantico, Virginia, to process the evidence. The investigators collected over four hundred DNA samples.

We asked the Knox County Sheriff's Department if they would work with a private detective. We were willing to pay any additional expense, but they declined. We were desperate for any way we could help further the investigation.

Change in Command

JJ Jones became the sheriff in 2007, replacing Tim Hutchison after years of service. Hutchinson had served more than his limit, so the commissioners sought a replacement.

I was excited about the change, but there wasn't a shift in the way Johnia's case was handled.

List of Prime Suspects

Jason Aymami

Jason was Johnia's friend and roommate. During their time at ETSU, they met when he dated one of her friends. Jason was twenty-three years old on the night Johnia died.

Jason was hospitalized for injuries he sustained during the attack. He had a wound near his eye and a sliced finger on his right hand. Later, I learned that he suffered a collapsed lung from one of the puncture wounds.

"Superficial" was the word some people used to describe his wounds. Next to what Johnia suffered, I guess I could understand why they felt that way. However, the mark on his face was very close to his eye, and a collapsed lung is anything but superficial. Jason's injuries were significant, and I'm glad he healed from them. He may have recovered physically, but I doubt the horror of that night will ever fully leave him.

After several months of finger-pointing and whispers, Jason moved to Colorado. Most people wondered if he was guilty and trying to flee, but now everyone knows he was running away from false accusations and derogatory remarks.

Jason gave a sketch artist details about the man who had attacked him. The artist drew a composite, and my husband and I circulated the image in hopes of capturing the person who murdered our daughter.

Key features on the sketch included the way the hair came to a peak, a stocky build, and almond-shaped eyes. We placed the picture on a billboard that ran along I-40 in hopes someone would recognize Johnia's murderer.

Sketch from Jason Aymami's description Courtesy of Knox County Sheriff's Department

Sometimes, detectives hold back certain information from the public. It's an effort to keep the guilty party from destroying evidence or realizing how close investigators are to discovering them. Other times, the decision is made by a supervisor, even though investigators want to release pertinent details to the media.

Almost a year later, the sheriff's office released photographs of the compact discs and the compact disc case found in the apartment and along the back steps. The public focused on the name of the album, "No Strings Attached", by the band NSYNC, claiming that it indicated my daughter's murder was a crime of passion. A CD recorded by the band Plan A was discovered, too, but it didn't lead the police any closer to her murderer, and no fingerprints were taken from the compact discs.

Jason was criticized for leaving Johnia in the apartment, but I hold no ill will toward him. He was attacked, and when he was able to phone for help, he asked the 9-1-1 operator to send someone to check on Johnia.

The police department asked Jason to take a polygraph test. He took the test willingly, and his answers never changed.

The man who administered the test told Jason that he failed. Jason was livid! It turned out the result was false; Jason passed. Jason wasn't responsible for Johnia's murder.

The insults and comments from the people around him were so upsetting that Jason moved to his brother's residence in Colorado.

After Jason Aymami left Knoxville and moved to Colorado, Mike and I went to visit him. I really wanted to talk with him again.

Jason told Mike and me the same story he had told the detectives. I'd seen the video the police took as they led him back through the apartment on the day of Johnia's funeral, but I listened attentively.

He said he came home that evening after working out at the gym. Johnia was sitting on the floor wrapping Christmas gifts she had purchased for some children.

Johnia went to bed around eleven or so and Jason went to his bedroom shortly afterward, falling asleep with his television on.

Around four in the morning, Jason said he heard sounds and thought Johnia was having a nightmare, but then he believed Johnia was screaming. Still thinking she was having a nightmare, he got out of bed to check on her.

He opened his bedroom door, and he saw a stocky man backing out of Johnia's room. The man shoved Jason back onto his bed and attacked him with the knife. The offender stabbed him in the face, chest, and hands. Jason said the only thing he remembered him saying was to "Shut up and be quiet!"

Jason caught a glimpse of the person from the light of the television. He was able to relay his mental image for a composite of the criminal.

He was able to get the assailant off him and make a run for it. He unlocked and opened the front door, ran down the stairs, and out into the dark, rainy morning. He never saw Johnia, and he thought she may have escaped while the perpetrator was stabbing him.

My husband and I are not upset with Jason. You never know what you would do if you were in that situation.

I helped Johnia move into the apartment. I spent time with her there and stayed overnight with her from time to time. I believed she'd be reasonably safe there if the doors were locked.

Jason Aymami

Before she was killed, Johnia and I had looked at other apartments. We were trying to find a place between the University of Tennessee and Peninsula Behavioral Hospital.

Rumors circulated about a romantic relationship between Johnia and Jason Aymami, but anyone who knew her wouldn't believe it. Jason and Johnia were friends—nothing more. Jason was just trying to help his friend until Johnia found a place of her own.

I don't think Jason has ever gotten over what happened the night Johnia died. It will leave him traumatized forever.

I haven't talked to Jason Aymami in years. I pray he's been able to heal physically, mentally, and emotionally, and I hope he receives the respect and treatment he deserves from the people around him.

Michael Perciful

The police received a tip about a group of people who were involved in a rash of robberies in the area. They brought in nineteen-year-old Michael Perciful and Detective Delgado was surprised when his shoes looked like they'd match a bloody shoeprint from the crime scene.

Even more surprising, he confessed to being part of the murder.

Detectives listened as he described my daughter's apartment, and they thought they finally had a true lead. He stated that Johnia and Jason were drug users who owed money to one of Perciful's associates. Perciful was left in the car when the drug dealer visited the apartment to collect the money, but he grew impatient. Perciful claimed that he entered the apartment and witnessed the dealer committing the murder.

His story had too many holes in it. Most notably, if Johnia and Jason were on drugs, why were their toxicology reports free of any and all drugs?

Perciful's fingerprints, DNA, and shoes were taken and evaluated, but none of them matched the evidence from the crime scene. Also, the more Perciful talked about the crime, the clearer it was that he was making up his involvement. His friend lived in an apartment in the same complex, so Perciful was able to describe the layout almost perfectly. However, as with most complexes, every other apartment is turned in another direction, so Perciful described the mirror image of Johnia's residence.

Michael Perciful

The authorities concluded that he wasn't involved in Johnia's murder. Perciful only wanted to be in the spotlight. He had wasted precious moments of the investigation with his false claims.

Noah Cox

Noah Cox and his friend, Taylor Olson, were at Cox's residence at Warren House Apartments on the night Johnia was murdered. They decided to steal a car, and given Noah's record, it wasn't an uncommon activity for him.

After grabbing a car stereo and some CDs, they tripped an alarm on one car and were separated as they ran away from the owner of the vehicle. The men ran in the rain with nothing to cover them but baseball caps.

Cox claimed that he passed out on his couch on the night my daughter was killed, and he didn't think anything of it when Taylor Olson was gone. It's hard for me to believe he was clueless about his friend's whereabouts.

Noah Cox

Olson's defense centered on the idea that Cox had killed Johnia. He tried to assuage his guilt in his suicide letter by saying Noah Cox had stabbed Johnia to death. Cox may be a repeat offender (and some would say a "career criminal"), but his DNA was not found in Johnia's apartment.

He probably knew something about Johnia's death, though. I heard Olson was scared to leave his room and he wouldn't watch television for a period of time after the incident. As his friend, Cox would have known the reason for Olson's behavior.

Cox has been in and out of jail, and my husband drove to his parole board hearings twice to speak against his release. Thankfully, he was not granted parole.

Additional People of Interest

Jason White

At the time of Johnia's death, Jason was her fiancé. Naturally, the police wanted to interview him, but we knew he could never hurt our daughter. Besides, he was miles away in Michigan when the murder took place. The detectives quickly crossed him off their list.

Tim and Kelly Burke

Time passed, and everyone was looking for a lead. Since no arrest was forthcoming, the Knoxville detectives had to explore every possible angle.

Everyone knew Johnia's two older brothers, Tim and Kelly, would never do anything to harm her, but the investigators had to look into everyone in Johnia's life. They had to be ruled out as suspects.

Tim and Kelly would have undergone any test to get closer to locating their sister's murderer. They would have accommodated any request from the Knox County Sheriff's Department.

I'm sure they had a good reason, but the Knoxville detectives drove over two hours to Tim's place of employment to collect his DNA. He was in the middle of his workday when they arrived.

I was baffled by this part of the investigation. Tim and Kelly would have willingly given their DNA to the investigators.

Perhaps they saw a reason to do it that way.

Of course, neither Tim nor Kelly's DNA matched the third set of DNA from the crime scene.

Augustine Joseph Leon

Leon was a confessed drug addict and friend of Olson and Cox. According to a statement Leon gave authorities, Cox admitted to killing Johnia during a botched burglary that Cox and Olson were carrying out at the apartment.

Leon described in his statement that Olson broke into what he thought was an unoccupied apartment, but my daughter and her roommate were there. When Olson started stabbing Johnia, Cox heard the commotion and ran to Olson's aid. Supposedly, he killed her as Olson ran away.

Three years after my daughter's murder, Leon's mother, Ruth Leon, came forward. She stated that she'd seen the sketch of my daughter's killer on a gas station newspaper and thought it looked like Noah Cox.

At the time of my daughter's murder, her son was in jail, and she asked him about it when she visited him. His path had crossed Noah Cox's, as Cox seemed to be in and out of jail. Her son told her that Cox had admitted to Johnia's murder.

It makes my head spin. *Why did she wait three years to come forward with the information?*

Sure, I'm glad she asked authorities to take another look at the case, but if she wasn't getting traction with law enforcement, why didn't she contact me at one of the community meetings or scheduled press interviews? The flyers were everywhere, and it's even possible that I placed one on Noah Cox's apartment door when I put flyers up at the complex where he lived.

Of course, since Leon was in jail at the time Johnia was killed, he was never a suspect, but he had information that could have significantly helped the case. If he did say something, I wish the lead would have been followed.

Putting more pressure on Noah Cox could have led us to Taylor Olson much faster!

Final Thoughts about the Suspects

Some of the leads came directly to us either through the blog or by phone. I directed all of the new information to Detective Brad Hall.

With each new lead, my stomach was tied in knots. My mind felt as though it was going to explode! I also understood with each new lead more time was needed to follow up on the new information.

For two years and ten months, finding the person that murdered my daughter was the only thing on my mind!

Detective Brad Hall with the Knox County Sheriff's Office was truly great about always returning my call. It meant so much to me, even without new information. His compassion for our situation helped me. Detective Hall assured me that he was following up on every piece of information he received and he was working on Johnia's case constantly. Detective Hall has a special place in my heart, and I will always be grateful for his work and kindness.

There were other suspects, but DNA doesn't lie. The killer's DNA was the only additional DNA found in Johnia's apartment. The evidence was in her bedroom, going out the back door, and down the steps. Also, his fingerprint and blood were on the murder weapon, and he admitted to killing her!

God answered my many, many prayers with the evidence against the killer and the DNA match. Many times after the murderer's arrest,

I would ask God how Mike and I, Johnia's brothers, and the rest of my family would make it through a trail.

I truly believe in my heart and mind that the person arrested for the crime did murder my daughter!

The laws in Tennessee have changed over the years and victims have more rights than they did nineteen years ago, but that does not extend to all murdered victims from many years ago. The Johnia Berry Act 2007 was the first step toward helping victims of violent crimes and their families, but there's still a long way to go.

Our hearts and prayers go out to all families who have lost loved ones to a violent crime and are continuing to fight for their justice.

The Coward's Way Out

On March 24, 2008, Olson was found in his jail cell. He'd hung himself by tearing his bedsheet and wrapping it around a clothes hook.

He wrote suicide letters, absolving his family from guilt over his actions and stressing that Noah Cox had murdered Johnia. The letters were delivered to his girlfriend, parents, and sister.

In response to Olson's death, I made a comment to the press. "It makes me angry. My daughter didn't get to leave a note. She didn't get to say goodbye."

At first, I was angry that he had taken a coward's way out, opting to hang himself with his bedsheet in his cell instead of facing the consequences of his actions. But then I thought about seeing him over the years, fighting against his parole, and possibly having him address me at his parole hearings, apologizing for an act from which I'd never recover.

Should he have continued to live and feel remorse for his actions, or was it better that he died, taking away his chances for small reprieves from his guilt while he was incarcerated? He stole my daughter's life from me, and he killed himself. That should be enough to prove his lack of respect for human life.

After getting the news that Taylor Olson hung himself in the Knox County Jail, I called the District Attorney General's Office to speak with the District Attorney General of Knox County. I asked the Attorney General if I could see Taylor Olson.

The Attorney General said, "What are you asking me, Mrs. Berry?"

I recall the exact words that I said to him. "I want to see Taylor Olson's dead body. I want to see him dead! It was just like the last time I saw my daughter. Dead because Taylor Olson brutally murdered her!"

The Attorney General told me that Taylor's body had already been sent to the coroner.

I replied, "I didn't think you would help me anyway. You think I'm just a crazy old woman!"

He assured me he didn't think that at all. He told me there were pictures from the scene and that the next time I was in Knoxville to let him know, and he would arrange for me to see the photographs.

It seemed crucial for me to see the murderer's dead body. I think it helped me to have closure in that part of the case.

It really bothered me to know that he had been walking free and enjoying the sunshine and all the pleasures of life. The pleasure that Johnia so loved and enjoyed. She loved sunny days so much!

You may say, "What if his family sees what you wrote?"

I wish them no harm. Also, I don't think they'll read my book. If they do, then they have made the reasonable assumption that I would not paint the murderer of my daughter well. He stole all her vibrant colors and left me in the darkness of mourning.

I saw the photos of Taylor Olson's dead body.

He would not be going to trial for the murder of Johnia. Unlike other families of victims, we were not dragged through the court system as we searched for justice.

Seeing his dead body didn't bring complete closure—I'll never have that—but it helped me move forward with my grief. As a parent, you are always your child's advocate, and I felt like it was up to me to help bring him to justice. I had an overwhelming need to see that Taylor Olson paid for the brutal murder of my only daughter.

Many folks have said to me, "It's sad you did not get justice."

In my heart, though, we did get justice. Taylor Olson's DNA was 6.8 billion to 1—a perfect match—to the blood found in Johnia's apartment. The fingerprint on the knife was a match, too. No matter what he said in his suicide letter, the facts don't lie

We are blessed that we don't have to repeatedly deal with the justice system, appeals, and parole hearings. I want to thank the District Attorney General for allowing me to see photos and for helping me put closure to *this* part of Johnia's murder.

A Word from Investigator Brad Hall

A cold, rainy night in December 2004 was a difficult time for a lot of people. It was hard for law enforcement, a family, a neighborhood, and a community.

I have been in law enforcement for thirty-five years, and it was the most horrific case I was involved in up to that time. I had been an officer for sixteen years when I started working on Johnia Berry's case.

During the next almost three years, I learned a lot about the victim, Johnia Berry, her family, her classmates, coworkers, and her friends. One of the most consistent things I heard was about Johnia's compassion and care, and she would always put others before herself. She loved kids and wanted to work with them when she got out of college.

It was a hard three years. We had a hard time locating suspects, but we worked diligently to find the one(s) responsible for the senseless death of this young lady. We communicated updates with the family daily to help keep them informed.

One summer day in 2007, all the hard work paid off. We were able to locate a suspect through DNA, and it was an unbelievable feeling for law enforcement. It was not as rewarding for the family—other than the suspect had been located. Now, they had to face possible years of court battles.

After months in jail, the suspect took his own life, leaving the family with the unanswered question about why he committed the heinous crime.

I will forever be impacted by Johnia and her family.

Captain Brad Hall
Knox County Sheriff's Department

Part Three

Johnia's Legacy

DNA

In 2007, the Johnia Berry Act was passed. It states that if a person is arrested in Tennessee for certain violent crimes, they must give a DNA sample.

It took two years to pass the law, and Tennessee was the eighth state to adopt it. There are still states that have not embraced the law, due to questions of constitutionality, but my hope is that all fifty states will enact the law soon.

It's just one step toward helping victims and their families receive justice, but it's an important one. If your state doesn't take DNA from violent offenders, you can help by writing legislative members.

After Johnia's murder, I couldn't think about anything except finding the person who murdered her. It was the only thing on my mind from the time I woke up until falling asleep at night. I didn't sleep a lot as my mind raced from one scenario to another, so I knew I had to find some way to get involved.

I was advised about the most effective way to appeal to legislators and move the Johnia's DNA Act forward. I printed post-cards with pre-printed words and added a picture of Johnia on her twenty-first birth-day to the front.

Joan and Mike Berry in front of a portrait of Joh-nia as a child

With some help, I collected thousands of signatures that supported a petition for Tennessee House Bill 2649 and Senate Bill 2651. The proposed bills required DNA testing of anyone arrested for a violent crime.

I gathered a group, and we met at my sister's house, hand-ad-dressed the cards, and prepared them to go to individual legislators. It was tedious, but our efforts were rewarded when the Johnia Berry Act was passed.

I cut the ribbon on Wednesday, July 8, 2009, at the grand opening of the Tennessee Bureau of Investigation's regional office and crime laboratory in Eastern Tennessee. It was a bittersweet day, and they quoted me on it. I told them, "Hopefully, this is going to help lots of other families who won't have to lose a daughter the way we lost Johnia."

Located off Strawberry Plains Pike, the 33,000-square-foot build-ing cost seventeen million dollars to erect. It serves twenty-one counties and screens for blood alcohol content, serology, toxicol-ogy, and DNA. It brought all the labs together in one place so they could share information more easily.

The Tennessee Bureau of Investigation dedicated the DNA lab to Johnia. It was a very touching tribute to her memory, and I know she'd be proud.

I am happy the new center allows an increased amount of DNA testing. Even though it can't bring back my daughter or the years we spent searching for her killer, it may help others.

Tennessee Bureau of Investigations,
Strawberry Plains, Tennessee
The Johnia Berry Act 2007

While working on DNA legislation in Georgia, we discovered they did not take DNA from convicted felons. "The Johnia Berry DNA Upon Conviction Act" was passed in Georgia in 2011. Georgia was the last of fifty states to take DNA upon a felony conviction.

Johnia Berry Toy Drive

On the night before her death, Johnia had been wrapping gifts for the children with whom she worked. No one was allowed in the apartment for months after the crime, so the detective gathered the gifts and gave them to us. We decided to deliver them.

The Johnia Berry Toy Drive has been active for almost two decades.

Every year, it provides a number of underprivileged children in Northeast Tennessee and Southwest Virginia with toys around Christmas.

Kay Ward has been with the toy drive for eighteen years.

The Johnia Berry Toy Drive stands as a remarkable testament to love's power and the lasting impact one person can have on her community and beyond. Johnia's spirit lives on through the annual holiday initiative which honors her love for children and serves those in need in Northeast Tennessee and Southwest Virginia. The drive serves as an enduring legacy, reminding us to cherish our loved ones, inspire future generations to a life of service, and care for each other in times of need. Whether it be in the form of a doll, board game, or even a shiny, new bicycle, the Johnia Berry Toy Drive is a beautiful holiday expression of love, compassion, and unity that year after year provides countless children the opportunity to unwrap a bit of hope and happiness on Christmas morning.

The toys are distributed to local charitable organizations on December sixth, the day Johnia's life ended. Johnia loved children, and part of her legacy is the spirit with which the toys are donated, gathered, and distributed. The night before her death, Johnia had wrapped presents for children. I believe she would have loved the idea and the happiness it has given to the children who received the toys from the drive.

**Johnia Berry Memorial Toy Drive
In Memory of Johnia and Her Love for Children
Annual contributions are accepted from November to December third of every year.**

FOOD CITY
Value. Everyday.
www.foodcity.com

FOR IMMEDIATE RELEASE

CONTACT: Tammy Baumgardner
K-VA-T Food Stores, Inc.
(276) 623-5100, Ext. 5734
(276) 623-5441, Fax
baumgardnertt@foodcity.com

**Food City to Host Annual
Johnia Berry Toy Drive**

ABINGDON, VA (Monday, October 30, 2017) – Food City will once again host the annual Johnia Berry Toy Drive. This marks the 12th year the retailer has hosted the memorial drive, which began in 2007.

"Johnia was extremely passionate about helping children and Food City is proud to be part of the annual Johnia Berry Toy Drive, which donates thousands of toys to needy children in our area each year," said Steven C. Smith, Food City president and chief executive officer.

The drive will kick-off on November 1st and continue through December 3rd. Specially marked collection containers will be located at area Food City locations throughout the Tri-Cities. The toys are scheduled to be distributed on December 6th, the anniversary of Johnia's death.

A number of local agencies receive the toys, including Haven of Mercy, Tri-State Children's Home, Safe Passage Women's Shelter, area schools in VA and TN, Cumberland Mountain Community Services and many others.

"We would like to thank our loyal customers and associates for their tremendous generosity and support of the toy drive, as well as our media partner, News Channel 11, WJHL-TV," adds Smith.

Headquartered in Abingdon, Virginia, K-VA-T Food Stores (Food City's parent company) operates 132 retail outlets throughout southeast Kentucky, southwest Virginia, east Tennessee, Chattanooga and north Georgia.

###

Johnia had taken a seasonal job at Zales jewelry store to purchase presents for the holiday season. When she got home the night before her death, she sat on the floor and separated the gifts she had purchased. She placed names on each gift and collected Christmas cards with Winnie the Pooh on them. They were precious gifts that she did not have the pleasure of giving to the children or the loved ones she treasured.

We were able to deliver the gifts to the children before Christmas. In honor of Johnia and her goal to devote her life to working with children, the toys are collected during the month of November and distributed to the organizations on the day Johnia was murdered, December sixth. The local agencies deliver the toys to needy children throughout East Tennessee and Southwest Virginia. December 6, 2022, marked the eighteenth year of the memorial toy drive. Food City grocery stores and News Channel 11, WJHL-TV have sponsored the Johnia Berry Toy Drive for eighteen years, making it possible to bring the joy of Christmas to thousands of less fortunate children.

Headquartered in Abingdon, Virginia, K-VA-T Food Stores (Food City's parent company), operates 147 retail outlets throughout Southeast Kentucky, Southwest Virginia, East Tennessee, North

Georgia, and Alabama. WJHL-TV News Channel 11 is the CBS news affiliate located in Johnson City, Tennessee. Throughout the years, the toy drive has grown tremendously, and so many volunteers have stepped up to make it a success.

(from left) Tim, Joan, and Kelly

Thanks to my sister, Patti, who has always supported the toy drive in so many ways. Truly, I could not have made it without her! I deeply appreciate Johnia's brothers, Tim and Kelly, for all their hard work.

Many volunteers put in countless hours to help organize the toys. Over the years, I have worked with some wonderful people, and I am thankful for them.

I am indebted to Pharoah's Car Club and the great friends that have repeatedly volunteered each year. Also, I extend special thanks to the public for their generous toy donations over the years. Your donations have brought hope and the joy of Christmas to less fortunate children. I send my love to all of you.

Christmas in July

In July 2023, BTAR (Bristol TN/VA Association of REALTORS) and Bristol Tennessee Schools put together a Christmas in July celebration in memory of my daughter. They helped the toy drive considerably by requesting each person who attended the street party bring a new, unwrapped toy for a child. BTAR is a wonderful group and Bristol Tennessee Schools are great, and I appreciate the time and effort they put into making it a special day.

The street was directly across from Tennessee High School in Bristol, where Johnia graduated from high school. I was happy to be so close to a place where my daughter made so many wonderful memories as a student, cheerleader, and friend. The area was decorated beautifully, and the homes reflected the Christmas season, with lights and festive yard adornments. The atmosphere was fun and inviting, and I was glad to be part of it.

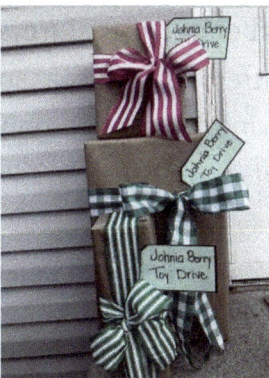

Food trucks were available, and games were set up for entertainment. It was a beautiful day, and it stayed busy.

It touched my heart that the representatives from BTAR chose the Johnia Berry Toy Drive for their donations. Tears sprang to my eyes when they told me that they planned to have the event every year.

HOPE Foundation and Advocating for Families of Murder Victims

HOPE for Victims was established after the murder of Johnia Berry in 2009 by Mike and me, and I'm the president of the foundation. HOPE's purpose is to speak on behalf of victims' rights, provide support groups for families and friends of victims of crime, increase public awareness to balance the scales of justice, and advocate for legislative initiatives that support our mission. Our mission includes equal rights for victims of crime and better tools for law enforcement.

HOPE for Victims has been instrumental in advocating for legislation for victims of crime. In 2007, the Johnia Berry Act was passed to promote DNA collection from offenders. This law helps by reducing investigation, prosecution, and court time. It also assists with plea bargains and cold cases and lowers state and local costs. In 2015, the Victim Life Photo Bill was passed, allowing photographs of murder victims as they appeared before their deaths to be shown during Tennessee murder trials.

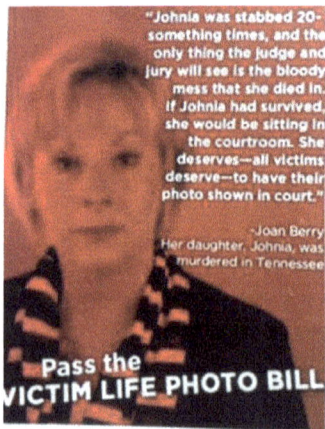

"Johnia was stabbed 20-something times, and the only thing the judge and jury will see is the bloody mess that she died in. If Johnia had survived, she would be sitting in the courtroom. She deserves—all victims deserve—to have their photo shown in court."

-Joan Berry
Her daughter, Johnia, was murdered in Tennessee

Pass the
VICTIM LIFE PHOTO BILL

Take a moment to think about it.

For some time before 2015, jurors didn't view a picture of the deceased while they were living. They were only subjected to pictures after the person had been killed.

What feelings does a picture of a dead body conjure up?

However, after the Victim Life Photo Bill was passed, an "appropriate" photograph of the victim during their life could be shown. It personalized the victim, and, hopefully, deepened the guilt the killer felt.

The defendant has a presence in the courtroom. He or she has a face and a voice. The Victim Photo Life Bill allowed victims the right to have their likeness shared before the crime took place.

Truth-In-Sentencing passed in 2022. It keeps those convicted of violent crimes like murders, carjackings, and vehicular homicides in prison for the duration of their sentence. Guilty parties must serve their full sentence without the possibility of parole or early release. Those convicted of lesser crimes, like aggravated assault, will be required to serve at least eighty-five percent of their time.

The foundation has had many outstanding victories! However, we have lost so much to get there. How many lives could have been saved if there were tougher penalties for violent crimes? How many murderers walked free before the Johnia Berry Act of 2007 was in place?

Each April, HOPE participates in National Crime Victims' Rights Week (NCVRW) by providing events to honor victims taken by violent crimes. I participate each year.

Families of the victims attend a vigil at the Knoxville Police Station. We hold the vigil at the beginning of National Crime Victims' Rights Week. People who have lost a family member due to a violent crime shared the names of their loved ones and when they died.

HOPE for Victims joins with Charme Allen, District Attorney General of Knoxville, Tennessee, to kick off NCVRW by honoring victims and the professionals who serve them. We pin attendees with a purple ribbon.

No one wants to be at the brick event because to be at that event means you've lost someone close to you due to a violent crime. Since the HOPE Foundation was established, we've seen some good things happen in legislation, but why did my daughter's death have to spur it? Why wasn't it already official?

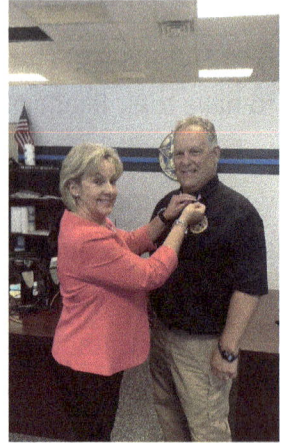

Joan Berry pinning Captain Brad Hall

September twenty-fifth is the National Day of Remembrance for Homicide Victims. It was recognized by the United States Senate in 2007.

HOPE for Victims hosts a Brick Memorial Service in remembrance of victims. It is held annually at City-County Building, on 400 Main Street, in Knoxville, Tennessee, on September twenty-fifth. Bricks may be purchased in memory of murdered family members.

It is a beautiful service, and they ring a bell for each victim. The silence is loud between the reading of each victim's name and gentle sobbing is not uncommon.

The State of Tennessee needs to enhance DNA collection to include all felony arrests. I keep working toward that goal, as I feel it's imperative for the safety of all Tennesseans.

Flyer for the Brick Memorial in 2022

Going to an event, such as the Brick Memorial Service, makes individuals more aware of struggles within the justice system. Sadly, victims' families can recount their difficulties as law enforcement officers located perpetrators, and they hoped to keep them incarcerated for the length of the guilty party's sentence.

During National Crime Victims' Rights Week, HOPE for Victims along with Sullivan County District Attorney General Barry Staubus and Debbie Locke (whose husband was murdered) hold a Victims of Violent Crimes Memorial in Blountville, Tennessee, at the Justice Center. We remember loved ones lost to violent crime. During this time each year, new names of crime victims are placed on the memorial. The Sullivan County Memorial gives a visual presentation for murder victims.

Our goal is to remember victims of violent crimes and raise awareness. Murdered victims don't have a voice now, so we have to be their voice. Victims need more rights, and I'm very passionate about establishing more rights for victims' families.

Debbie Locke, who lost her husband due to a drunk driving hit-and-run, and I raised over $8,000 for the memorial. We hoped it would help support the friends and families who lost a loved one to violent crimes.

At the time I took the picture, there were twenty-three names on the memorial. Johnia's name was listed.

Victims of Violent
Crimes Memorial

Alongside the District Attorney General Offices, HOPE for Victims hosts Holiday Remembrance Services during December. The services are held in Knoxville, Blountville, and Jonesborough, Tennessee. We remember the victims of violent crimes. Family and friends of victims attend the services to honor their loved one(s) by hanging a special ornament on the tree. Some ornaments are handmade with love by family members.

HOPE for Victims provides a series of supportive books for children, teens, and families on their journey of grief. The book series is called HOPE for Children and Families, and they are free. When families find the support they need, it helps the entire family cope and understand they can stay close, even though the feelings of grief may be very strong. For more information, please contact hopeforvictims.org or LaVerne Craig at (865) 924-3480.

We hold monthly meetings. You may join us for our monthly support meeting at

Grace Presbyterian Church
1610 Midpark Road
Knoxville, Tennessee

You can find us there every second Wednesday of each month at 6:30 PM.

HOPE attends parole hearings to advocate on behalf of crime victims. Over the years, I have been asked to testify at a number of parole hearings to support victims of violent crime.

A parole hearing is a hearing to determine whether an inmate should be released from prison to parole supervision in the community for the remainder of the sentence. A Hearing Examiner of the United States Parole Commission conducts the hearing. The decision on whether the inmate should be granted parole is made by a Commissioner of the United States Parole Commission after reviewing the hearing record created by the Hearing Examiner.

The best way to ensure that you will receive notice of parole hearings is to register for the Federal Victim Notification System. Among other things, the automated database notifies victims about prisoner releases.

A victim or the family may appear in person at the institution where an inmate is confined or via video from a United States Attorney's Office and offer a statement during the hearing. A victim may also submit a written or recorded statement to the Commission in before of the hearing. In addition, a victim may request permission to present an oral statement.

When a representative of HOPE and/or the victim testify at the parole hearing, it feels as though we are begging the parole board for justice. The victims and family members of victims have to relive the crime every time a parole hearing is scheduled.

HOPE asks the parole board to deny parole for the inmate and delay the next parole hearing for as long as the law allows. We let them know the severity of the crime and the impact the crime has had on victims, their families, and the community. If they decide to grant parole, we hope the parole board considers the safety of the family members and the community.

When the hearing is over, there is a time period of up to fourteen days before victims and/or their families know the decision of the parole board. This is not justice! Victims do not get a second chance!

A board member of HOPE for Victims, LaVerne Craig whose mother, Dollie Odom Gouge, was murdered in 1987, has been to three parole hearings in 2008, 2014, and 2020. Another hearing looms ahead in 2026. LaVerne said:

I've been involved with the justice system for thirty-five years. I've been to three parole hearings—with another approaching in a couple of years—and hundreds of court hearings.

I guess you could say I have a love/hate relationship with the justice system. I love that it brought justice for my mother's murder, but I hate it for continuing to give so many rights to the perpetrator of the crime and continuing to re-victimize me with no end in sight.

As a victim of a crime, how do I ever truly heal? I don't; healing and closure are empty words that do not exist.

Recently, I have helped in the efforts to pass Marsy's Law in the State of Tennessee. The House passed it, but the law will reach the Senate soon.

What is Marsy's Law? Marsy's Law was passed to honor Marsalee (Marsy) Ann Nicholas, who was stalked and murdered by her ex-boyfriend in 1983. On the way home from the funeral service, Marsy's family stopped at a store. In the checkout line, only one week after her daughter's murder, Marsy's mother was approached by her daughter's murderer. She had not been notified of his release, and the family was unaware he had posted bail only days after Marsy's murder.

Unfortunately, there are many similar stories.

Marsy's Law was established to give rights to victims of crimes and families of murder victims. These individuals could choose to receive a notification upon the release of the accused, and the law gives them the right to be heard and get notified about criminal proceedings.

I'm grateful to State Representative Patsy Hazlewood and Senator John Stevens for their help with Marsy's Law. I hope during the next legislative session that the Senate supports the law so victims of violent crimes and the families of murder victims will have the rights they deserve.

Captain Brad Hall of the Knox County Sheriff's Department had this to say about the HOPE Foundation:

H – **H**elp
O – **O**thers
P – **P**ersevere
E – **E**ncourage

Joan Berry and Captain Brad Hall

"I'm proud to be a board member of this great organization that helps victims of crimes and their families deal with the tragedy in their lives. The foundation holds monthly support group meetings and there are several events throughout the year to help honor the lost loved ones. (Toy Drive, Victim's Remembrance Tree, Brick Memorial, Victim's Rights Week, etc.)

The organization has been instrumental in getting legislation passed by going to Nashville and speaking with legislators about laws to protect victims. Today, the organization continues to go to Nashville on behalf of victims."

An Angel Named Johnia

In 2022, Jocelyn Lacey, Johnia's sorority mentor and dear friend, wrote a children's book about Johnia. It talked about her hopes and dreams and mentioned her death, but the book didn't discuss the act that put her in heaven. In the book, God explains to Johnia that she made a lasting contribution, and she was still in the hearts of her family and friends.

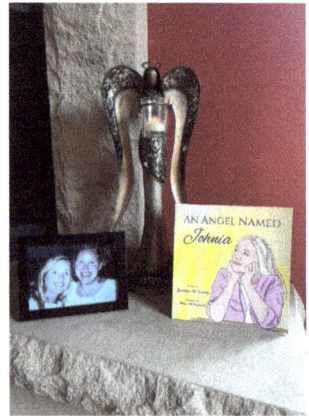

Jocelyn M. Lacey's book and a picture of her with Johnia

Jocelyn bought a pink candle, as Johnia's favorite color was pink. The name of the candle is *Snowflake Kisses*. Jocelyn said, "I had the label made for Joan for the anniversary of Johnia's death for her birthday in Heaven." It made her think of Johnia blowing snowflake kisses from Heaven.

Johnia's death was hard on everyone she knew, and we all seem to remember exactly where we were when we heard the news. Jocelyn was no different.

Jocelyn had this to say:

"I was living in Indianapolis, Indiana, and working for my sorority headquarters when I learned of Johnia's death from a fellow sorority sister of ours down in Tennessee. I remember being in total disbelief that this happened—not only that Johnia had died young at the age of twenty-one, but that her life was taken in such a brutal, violent way.

"I called one of my best friends, Steven Lacey (who later became my husband), who had also known Johnia and whose friend had dated her in our college days. He immediately told his friend, Sami, and both of them went to her funeral. It pained me that I could not attend due to the distance, but I felt that Steven was my representative there.

"I did not know Joan prior to Johnia's death. I made a financial gift to our sorority foundation in Johnia's memory and heard from Joan once the acknowledgment had been sent. We developed a close friendship and on the one-year anniversary of Johnia's death, with her murder still unsolved, Joan asked me if I would speak at a vigil they were planning to have at the private family cemetery where Johnia was buried.

"The media had been invited to attend in order to keep Johnia's case in the spotlight. We hoped the killer would be found and arrested and we could finally get justice for Johnia.

"I was honored to be asked to speak and started planning what I would say. In my speech, I communicated the difficulty of the day as it was the anniversary of Johnia's death. I told everyone I liked to think of that painful day as her birthday in Heaven. We all have an earthly birthday; the day we come into the world, and it somehow helped on that painful day for her family and friends to look at December sixth as her heavenly birthday. Now, she is with her Lord and Savior and is eternally safe from any other evil that could harm her.

"When Joan asked me to help with the Johnia Berry Holiday Toy Drive in Johnia's memory the following year, I enthusiastically said, 'Yes!' Her mission was to help give children in Northeast Tennessee and Southwest Virginia a Christmas they deserved in Johnia's memory. New and unwrapped toys could be donated by the community and dropped off at area Food City grocery stores throughout November and be donated to area nonprofit organizations on December sixth, the anniversary of Johnia's death.

"She had the idea to start the toy drive in Johnia's memory as her Christmas present to Johnia, as Johnia had spent the last night of her

life buying and wrapping Christmas presents for the special children in her life. Johnia had also planned a career to help children.

"I was working at a domestic violence shelter at the time, and some of the toys went to children who were in the shelter. I later worked at a children's advocacy center and toys also went to those children, as well as numerous others in the Northeast Tennessee and Southwest Virginia regions. I was so honored to be a part of the toy drive each year until I moved out of the area.

"I remember the day that Johnia's murderer was arrested. It was a fall day in September 2007, a little over two years and ten months since Johnia's death, and I had just placed my order at Panera Bread in Johnson City.

"My cell phone started ringing and it was my husband, Steven. I had asked him earlier if he'd wanted me to pick up anything for him from Panera while I was there. Thinking that he had changed his mind and wanted me to get something for him, I answered his call while I was still at the register in case I needed to add anything to the order. Instead, he told me that an arrest had been made in Johnia's murder case. In total disbelief that this day had finally and prayerfully come, I loudly repeated what he had just shared with me, not realizing or caring if I was making a scene. I had been the one to tell him of Johnia's death and now he was the one telling me of the arrest that had finally come.

"The perpetrator had been arrested for another crime, and the DNA that he submitted matched the DNA at the crime scene of Johnia's murder. All I could do was rejoice and thank God that this day had finally come!

"There was no trial because the person accused of Johnia's murder committed suicide in jail. He wrote a suicide note, pointing the finger at someone else, which we all knew was a lie because his DNA had matched what was found at the crime scene for Johnia's murder. And if it had been someone else, as he claimed, there would have been no reason to kill himself. It was widely believed that he had taken the cowardly way out and would not answer for the crime he had committed. We would never know why or what Johnia's last moments were because the person who knew (if he could even be trusted to tell the truth) had chosen to end his life.

"When I talked to Joan after learning this fact, she was initially angry because he wouldn't have to answer for the beautiful life he had taken. He had written instructions for his funeral, like what songs he wanted to be played and etcetera when Johnia didn't have that opportunity.

"Years later, it appeared to be a blessing that he had taken his life. The family was spared from sitting at his parole hearing every so often and having to see the perpetrator who brutally took their daughter's life while making their case on why he never needed to see the light of day.

"They were spared from that and knowing many families didn't have that same privilege, Joan was instrumental in passing another law called "Truth in Sentencing" in the state of Tennessee. It states that perpetrators who are found guilty in a court of law have to serve 100% of their sentences. She also orchestrated the "Johnia Berry DNA Act" passed in 2007. It states that a person who is arrested for a violent felony will have a biological specimen taken for the purpose of DNA analysis. If this DNA law had been in place before Johnia's death, her murderer would have either been in jail for the other crimes he had committed, and Johnia would still be alive or he would have been caught much sooner due to his DNA matching the blood at the crime scene.

"Joan also helped pass the "Photo Bill" that states that a victim's picture can be shown in court as they were shortly before their death instead of only the crime scene pictures of them. Joan has tiredly advocated for these changes and has truly made all the difference in the world. She is truly an inspiration and I know Johnia is so proud of her and is smiling down on her, giving her strength to make it through another day."

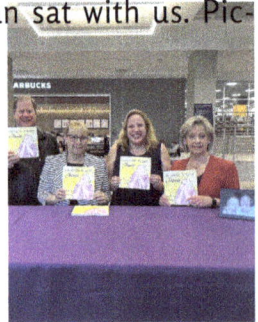

(From left) Mike and Joan Berry and Jocelyn and Steven Lacey

Jocelyn and I attended several book signings for *An Angel Named Johnia*. We went to Johnia's alma mater, East Tennessee State University, Barnes & Noble in Johnson City, and the Alcoa Library. The Alcoa Library in Bristol, Tennessee, had a special place for Johnia's book.

At ETSU, the dean sat with us. Pictured right, Jocelyn sent a photo of Dr. Wallace Dixon, Chair and Professor of Psychology at ETSU's College of Arts & Sciences, Denise Asbury, Director of Development of ETSU's College of Arts & Sciences, herself, and me on ETSU's campus for the book signing of An Angel Named Johnia.

Impact on the Family

When Tim and Kelly arrived at the Knoxville hospital, Kelly said they were there for a while before they identified Johnia's body. I'm now—and have always been—upset that the hospital did not wait until Mike and I arrived to identify Johnia's body. We were her next of kin!

Having the boys identify Johnia's body was an excruciating, spearing pain that they will live with for the rest of their lives! Even though they only viewed a photo of Johnia attached to a clipboard, the image of her in death will be seared into their minds. Her beautiful blonde hair was soaked with blood, and her usually unblemished face was covered with blood. The startling photograph has left an ever-lasting terrifying picture in their minds of their beautiful sister, who always had an infectious smile. I wish that I could have spared them that pain. It saddens my heart that they have to live with that terrible memory forever.

Years ago, Kelly wrote about Johnia's death and his feelings. *From, Eddie* is his contribution to the book. Even though he wrote it over a decade ago, I can't ask him to revisit the most traumatic experience of his life.

Tim chose to provide something for the book. His words remind me of how protectively he watched over Johnia and the love he has for his family.

Tim Burke, Johnia's Brother

Just short of publishing this book about my sister Johnia, my mom, Joan Berry, asked if I would like to add something. I was torn about writing anything at all.

My sister was cheated out of living a long life and having a family of her own. I think back to her childhood and how she would be waiting for me to get home from school. When I got off the bus, she would yell, "Mimmy," because she couldn't call me Timmy yet.

Johnia was so very sweet and caring. She was extremely successful as she moved through her adolescence and into her teen years.

I know without a doubt she would have been a great mother. I know this because she was already a wonderful aunt to my children Camryn, Cassidy, and Cadyn.

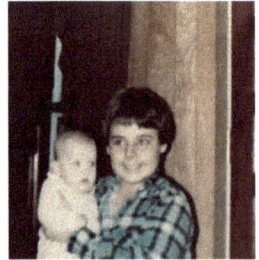
Johnia and Tim

Partially, I was torn about writing something for the book because my sister loved my children so very much. My children were deprived of knowing such a wonderful person. I see Johnia's traits in my children and only wish that they would have had more time to know their Aunt Johnia.

I wish that my wife, Melissa, and her children would have had the opportunity to spend time with her.

I'm aware of the pain and loss that my sister's early death caused my family. I grew up spending much of my childhood with my grandfather, Warren. I admired him. I only remember seeing him cry one time in my life, and that was at Johnia's funeral.

I pass my sister's picture in the hall daily, and I only have memories and thoughts of what could have been. I could write so much more, but those memories are mine and I cherish the time I had with her on this earth. For that, I will keep those with me.

I will always love and miss my little sister.

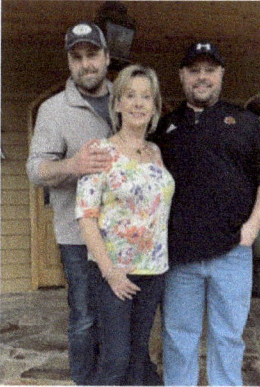

(from left) Kelly, Joan, and Tim

I'd like to share some things about my mom. I know that this is not what she intended for me to do, but I am going to mention her.

My mother's love and devotion for her children can never be denied. I knew from a very early age how much she cared for her children. It's evident now, more than ever.

I know how devastating Johnia's death and the years that followed it were for my mom. I wish that I could take away all the heartache and suffering she has endured for the past twenty years, but I can't.

What I can tell you is about my mother's tenacity. She has fought for the rights of victims and their families. She has met with people and sponsored legislation to help those who no longer can speak for themselves. She has held and sponsored a toy drive for children that my sister wanted to help. She has kicked down doors that would have never been previously opened.

(from left) Joan and her son, Tim

My mom is truly a hero, and for that, I will always be in awe. Thank you for being a great mother.

From Patti Baker, Johnia's Maternal Aunt

Joan Berry and Patti Baker

Johnia's light was one so special and warm that instead of dimming in death, it burned even brighter. Through her beautiful and vibrant memory, the Grace of God, and the labors of her family and those close to her, Johnia has seen the faces of hundreds of children glow on Christmas morning.

Johnia has also ensured justice for victims' rights, Truth-In-Sentencing, and the creation of a DNA database in Tennessee.

Johnia's murder was a senseless tragedy, yet she has continued to be remembered for the beautiful person she was.

My Grandchildren

When they were young, Camryn, Cassidy, and Cadyn had come to visit. We were on our way home from the amusement park and stopped to pick up a pizza. Mike got out of the car and went inside.

Cassidy said, "Nana, are the doors locked? We have to make sure the doors are locked because of what happened to Johnia!"

Camryn spoke up, "Cassidy, don't say that! It makes Nana sad."

After you lose a loved one to murder, you become more aware of your surroundings and, at times, you become anxious. Life has forever changed, and you will always live with it. It's constantly in my subconscious mind to make sure nothing like what happened to Johnia happens again.

I want my grandchildren to live life to the fullest, though. My granddaughters are bright, beautiful women who have accomplished and will accomplish many achievements, and my grandson has a beautiful heart.

Will their aunt's death touch their decisions in life? In some ways, it always will. It's unavoidable.

They will definitely double back to be certain they locked their doors. However, I hope they're always as adventurous and full of life as Johnia.

Her legacy lives on in the Johnia Berry Act 2007 and in the hearts of the ones who loved (and still love) her.

I have very sweet memories of Camryn and Johnia. Camryn always wanted to ride in Johnia's convertible car; she loved it! Sometimes, she just would just sit in the car with the top down and wave to us.

Aunt Johnia and Camryn

Camryn, Johnia's Niece/ Tim's Daughter

"You can't live your life in fear."
I repeat that to myself every day. Every morning, every night, every trip to the grocery store, every time I walk alone in a parking lot, and every time I travel to an unfamiliar place. Every single day.

I was only five years old when my Aunt Johnia was murdered. As I got older, I was more curious about what really happened to her. I was a young woman, and I wanted to know all the details. But what I really wanted to know was: How can I protect myself from the same fate?

I read, watched, and researched. I experienced uneasiness after I discovered the true brutality of her death. My mind was constantly rummaging through thoughts, like Where did that person come from? Are the doors locked? Is my Instagram still set to private? I believed that living a more guarded life would lessen my chances of suffering the same fate as my aunt.

After some time, I was frustrated with those thoughts. I had talked with many of the people that I loved and trusted the most, and they shared the same advice: "You can't live your life in fear."

My perception of that phrase as well as my obedience to it changed when Mike Berry said it to me. Mike, my grandfather and Johnia's dad, said it. The same person who had lost his own daughter to a horrific murder.

*The conversation went something like this: "You can't live your life in fear because you are **not living**. Do what makes you happy in life." In that pivotal moment, I came to the realization that I had not been **living life to the fullest**.*

*So, from that moment, I reminded myself that I cannot live my life scared and fearful. Instead, I have to live smartly and with caution. But **I have to live**.*

Johnia's short life—and love for life—proved to me that I must live my life to the fullest because things can change in an instant. I know she will want to hear about all of my adventures when I meet her in heaven one day, so I cannot let fear hold me back. She would want me to truly live.

I love and miss you, Aunt Johnia... until we meet again.

Love,

Camryn

I remember something special about Johnia and my granddaughter, Cassidy. Johnia gave Cass a little yellow stuffed bear when she was two years old. Cassidy loved that bear, played with it, and slept with it every night. "Yellow Bear" was so well loved that it started to get a little ragged. Cassidy's grandmother, Donna, repaired it several times before its arm completely detached. Cassidy still has Yellow Bear and plans to pass it on to her children. It brings a smile to my lips every time I think of the beloved toy passing to another happy child.

From Cassidy Burke, Johnia's Niece/Tim's Daughter

Emily Dickerson once wrote, Hope is the thing with feathers, that perches in the soul, and sings the tune without the words, and never stops at all. *Johnia Hope, my aunt, a daughter, a granddaughter, a sister, a cousin, and a loved one was taken from my family too soon. However, her memory will forever have life.*

My memories of Johnia are not very numerous as I was young when she passed away; however, the stories, memorials, and pictures of my aunt speak a thousand words. The tragic death of my aunt is often something an individual thinks will "never happen to my family." I think it is safe to say my family believed that, too, until that December day.

Johnia and Cassidy

The day my aunt died was the day that every-thing in my family changed. We learned to love unconditionally, always fight for justice, hold our loved ones close, and always check our blindside. We had to learn how not to walk in fear, but rather to walk in courage, faith, and bravery. Johnia's life is remembered daily, especially around every December as my family hosts a Johnia Berry Memorial Toy Drive. I have been fortunate enough to be a part of the drive for many years and give back to local communities and children, as that is what my aunt loved. As Emily Dickerson wrote, [hope] never stops at all. Johnia's memory and life will forever be alive within my family. Johnia Hope, splendid with feathers, you have your angel wings. Until we meet again, I hope you continue to dance in heaven.

With love,
Cassidy

I have a precious memory of Johnia and Cadyn.
Johnia was so excited on the day of Cadyn's birth. She got to the hospital before I did. She got to see and hold Cadyn before I did, and she always loved teasing me about it.

From Cadyn Burke, Johnia's Niece/Tim's Daughter

Johnia and Cadyn

I was just a year and a half old when my aunt was tragically taken from my family. I was robbed of the chance to truly get to know her, but my family has always kept her memory alive. Even though I never got the chance to make my own memories with Johnia, I am grateful for the stories

I can't say my aunt's passing has changed my life, but what I can say, is her death has shaped my life. I was raised by a family that gave back to our community and worked hard to make the world a better place—two things that helped create the person I am today. While I will always wonder how different my life would be if Johnia was still with us, I know she is proud of everything my grandparents and family have done despite their sadness.

Johnia, I like to think you are watching over us and protecting us each day. We will miss you every day until we meet again.

Love,
Cadyn

Even though he never got to know her, I have special memories of Quinn when I think about Johnia. Quinn always says, "I wish I could have known Aunt Johnia."

I wish he could have known her, too. She would have loved him so much! Maybe they could have watched Transformers together or ridden around in her convertible.

Quinn always loved helping with the toy drive. He enjoyed collecting the toy from the barrels.

One year, Quinn attended the Victims Remembrance Tree Ceremony at the City County Building in Knoxville, Tennessee. Victims' families were present at the ceremony. They announced the name of their loved one and hung an ornament on the tree.

This particular year, Quinn asked if he could announce Johnia's name. He went to the podium, took the microphone, and said, "I'm here to remember my aunt, Johnia Berry. Then, he went over to the tree and hung her ornament. It was a very special moment for me.

**From Quinn Burke Johnia's Nephew/
Kelly's Son**

Johnia Berry...

Personally, I don't know much about my aunt and what she did for others, but I do know that she was a wonderful person with a very kind heart. I wish I could have met her. It would have been a delight.

Johnia's death was very tragic for my family. My dad and uncle were the two siblings of my dear Aunt Johnia. They have been in great pain since her death, but I try to stay strong for them.

My grandmother has developed a toy drive for my aunt called the Johnia Berry Toy Drive. The toy drive helps kids who are in need of care and love, and the toy drive will give them toys. I have helped out a few times, and it is special for us and for others.

We are a Christian family and pray to the LORD about Johnia every August twenty-sixth (the birthday of Johnia) and December sixth (the date of Johnia's death). Even though she isn't here with us right now, she is still my aunt, and I will still love her like anyone else in my family.

Thank you and God bless.

Kelly and Quinn at the Johnia Berry Toy Drive

Kristie Riddle (mother of Johnia's three nieces)

There are many things in life that change us. Sometimes, the changes are for the good. Sometimes, they are not. Sometimes, perhaps, they are a little of both.

Johnia's untimely and unnecessary death changed me. It changed the way I saw the world and the people in it, have parented my three daughters, walked through the world, and learned to appreciate and value life.

When Johnia was killed, I was a young mother of three very young daughters. With her death, I not only lost her and experienced all the grief that comes with such a loss, but I also lost a sense of peace, freedom, and security that I had taken for granted in my life. Everything looked and felt different to me, and even my own home didn't feel safe anymore. I moved from feeling confident about safely raising my children, to a place of fear, uncertainty, and a feeling of being on the lookout for the inevitable worst to happen. That place is an uncomfortable and scary one, and all these years later, I find myself still there, praying to stay one step ahead of it.

Losing someone you love in a violent way changes you. The change is permanent.

Thankfully, and with much intent, I have experienced a few good changes in my life that resulted from Johnia's death, sowing positive seeds in the world. The annual toy drive has been an incredible success and touched many lives. It is a reminder that I am thankful for many things. I'm thankful for it. My daughters are thriving and healthy, making their mark on the world. I'm thankful for that, too. Actually, the list I have of things to be grateful for is quite long. Appreciating that is not lost on me.

Johnia, until I see you again, much love.

Kathy Brown (my dear friend)

I met Johnia when she was sixteen months old. Her mother, Joan, and I had a business together, and we became good friends.

I remember, when I met her, Johnia had a cast on her leg because she had climbed out of her crib.

When Johnia was young, I was around her a lot. I taught school, and since she went to kindergarten near where I worked, she rode with me. We were together every school day in the morning and afternoon. Each time we drove forty-five minutes, and she climbed independently into the back seat.

She looked like a princess every day and talked in a mature, adult-like manner. It was years before her time as she was only five!

Underneath her prim and proper beauty, Johnia was intelligent, vibrant, and a spitfire of a little girl! She always talked about her friends *with deep seeded emotions that depicted love and care for them. She never ran out of things to say!*

I get very saddened because I can still see her beautiful little face, and I always remember her infectious smile. When evening came, she was eager to tell me about her day.

Sweet little Johnia grew up to be a beautiful young lady. She always stayed sweet with her same infectious smile and was extremely intelligent. Most of all, though, she had the biggest heart full of love and caring for others. I feel the greatest gift to all those who knew her was love.

I miss her deeply and think of what she was going to do in life, the people she would have helped, the people she loved. Mostly, I think of the difference she would have made in the lives of all those who would have been blessed to have known her.

Johnia was ambitious, adventurous, and determined to make a difference!

I am heartbroken over her absence because it has taken away so much love and happiness from her loved ones and the world.

Moving Forward

Days turned into weeks and months into years. Johnia's murder was the only thing on my mind every waking minute. There were lots of hours spent alert because sleep didn't come easy or often. I had to stay busy, I constantly thought of things I could do to keep Johnia's case alive and active.

Holidays came and went. The first Christmas without Johnia was unbearable. I visited her grave and took a small Christmas tree with me. I placed angels and purple and pink decorations on the artificial branches. Around Christmas every year, I put the tree back up and decorate it in memory of Johnia.

I kept her wedding dress and the bridesmaids' dresses. They should have been worn on April 30, 2005, but they hang in my closet. It took a long time before I could attend a wedding. All I could think of was the wedding my daughter missed.

We kept her convertible. Maybe I can part with it one day, but I doubt it. Just like the dresses, the car represents so much of an unfinished life.

Mother's Day is always a hard day. Tim and Kelly make the day special for me. I know they go out of their way to be with me on that day, and I appreciate it more than they will ever know. Simply being near them is enough.

During the investigation, I called Tim and Kelly frequently to keep them updated. I didn't realize that I wasn't there for them to help them deal with the anguish of losing their only sister to murder.

One day, Tim and I were talking, and I expressed I couldn't bear life without Johnia. He softly said, "Mom you still have Kelly and me."

I can still hear those words. I thought, *God what have I been doing? You have blessed me with two other children, and I have been selfishly thinking only of myself and my pain—not being a mom that Tim and Kelly could talk to about their sister or express their pain and other feelings.*

They stayed silent because they didn't want to burden me as I experienced the worst pain of my life. From the bottom of my heart, I apologized to both of them.

I'm sorry for their pain, and I'm so sorry for not being there for them. I'm sorry for not being the mom I should have been through

Kelly and Tim Burke

their grief. I love both of them dearly and thank God for them.

We were all blessed to have Johnia in our lives for twenty-one years, and I am blessed to have my sons, grandchildren, and step-grandchildren in my life, too.

Living without your treasured loved ones is one of the hardest things a person can do. Waking up with the realization that I'd never see my daughter again hurts me every day. I don't wish that pain on anyone.

(from left) Johnia, Joan, and Mike Berry

Johnia's wedding would have taken place on April 30, 2005. Johnia and I went to wedding venues, and she selected a beautiful gown that I keep in my closet. At this point, I still can't imagine letting anyone wear it, and I avoided weddings for years. It was just too hard.

I don't like sunny days because she loved sunny days, and they remind me of Johnia's bright personality. Rainy days are hard, too, as it was raining on the day we buried her and pouring on the day she died. The angels were coating us with their tears.

My husband and I still have Johnia's convertible. Her cap and gown and the wedding dress she would have worn at her April wedding still hang in our closet. We have her phone, and we recorded her voicemail message.

We hold Johnia dear to our hearts, but we continue to live. We don't let fear define our lives, but we will never be the same without our darling daughter.

When Johnia's friend, Jocelyn, was asked about moving forward after Johnia's death, she replied, "The best gift we can give Johnia is to live our lives the best way we can to honor her and her memory and to be her voice. She touched so many lives in her short time on Earth and her legacy continues in helping other people through advocacy, the toy drive, and changing laws that will make people safer."

Mike Berry

My Blessing Named Johnia

The day that Johnia and I started our journey together was the greatest day of my life. Johnia, who I nicknamed Dude, and I was her Mikey. She was the sweetest, kindest, and most loving person in the world.

We had such a great relationship from her childhood to adulthood. She was so mature for her age.

I have so many memories of her school, dance, cheer, high school, Top Gun Cheerleading, and ETSU. I remember her first Disney World experience, cruise, beach trip. Anything "family" was with Johnia involved.

from right: Johnia and her dad, Mike Berry

I remember Chiquita her Chihuahua dog. She loved that little dog.

When Johnia went to college, she set so many goals and worked very hard. During the last summer of her undergraduate degree, she took seven classes to get her second degree in criminology.

I used to go to visit her at ETSU during the week to take her—and sometimes a friend—out to dinner. Those are special memories for me.

When she was in elementary school, we would have one night a week that was just our date night, we would go to dinner. Her mom would be working late, and sometimes join Johnia and me. Johnia was so adorable and funny, she would say to her mom, this is our date night!!

In one of my memories, Joan and I took Johnia and a friend to a Matchbox Twenty concert. The venue was the World's Fair Park in Knoxville, Tennessee. When we picked her up, she told us that she body surfed.

I still listen to Matchbox Twenty's music and think of the concert we shared with Johnia.

Johnia loved music and had many CDs. I think that's how I stay in touch with her. Every day I listen to "Angles Among Us" by Alabama and "See You Again" by Charlie Puth.

Johnia made a difference in this world before and after she was taken.

I hope to "see you again". I still think of you and love you every day, Johnia.

Love,

Dad (Mikey)

Johnia's Legacy Continues

Friends and Coworkers Who Have Memories of Johnia

Johnia touched the lives of so many people. I can't count the number of well-meaning people who shared a memory of my precious daughter with me.

Sadly, the pressure of my grief was so great that I may miss someone who spoke words that moved me to tears. On Johnia's memorial page, I asked for memories of my daughter. I have placed their recollections in this section.

If you don't see something you've spoken to my family or written on the message board, I'm sorry. Every memory of Johnia is precious to me, and I will store them in my heart. I have shared these memories with special permission.

A young lady, Jessie, who had worked with Johnia at the Peninsula Hospital, contacted me through Facebook Messenger. She said that Johnia used to work an early shift with her, and Johnia brought "breakfast" for them in the form of two Reese's Cups. Johnia bought a twin pack and claimed that she could only eat one. Knowing it was her coworker's favorite treat, she offered her the other one. She brought the Reese's Cups every day she worked with the other young woman.

The story was dear to me. Johnia and I loved to eat Reese's Cups.

My fondest memory of Johnia was when my daughter, Kendra, babysat her. She loved Johnia, and the feeling was mutual. Johnia would have made a wonderful teacher and mother. Also, she and I shared birthdays which made her special to me. Johnia was beautiful inside and out.

I met Johnia through her beautiful mom. Even though we don't see each other often, I love her and consider her a friend. It has always saddened me that a beautiful girl had her life shortened by such a monster, and I am sorry that he was not punished for his awful crime."
— Brenda Honaker

I can't name just one memory of Johnia, but if I had to, I'd say it would be the beach trip. Every memory I have of her is special and will never leave my heart. I miss her every day. I hope you and Mikey are doing well and your family is healing.
— Katie Bacon

The memory that I have of Johnia is staying at your [Johnia's] house. We went to Pigeon Forge to her brother's wedding and then to Damon's to eat afterward. We also cheered together in school.
— Tommie Ashley

I think it's so wonderful that you are writing a book about Johnia. She truly was a precious young woman.

I wanted to share with you a memory I have of her. I went to school with her from middle school up but really only became friends with her in the eleventh grade in Mr. Depriest's English class. We were assigned in alphabetical order seating.

I didn't know her very well, at first, but I will never forget how kind she was to me and how fast we became friends. I'll also never forget how kind she was to my friends as soon as she met them.

She was always so giving. I remember she bought popcorn at the movies once for a friend of mine that she had just met because she didn't have the money for it. Such a good friend and a wonderful person through and through. Surely, I will never forget her.
— **Misty Arnett Seal**

I remember Johnia's hugs. She was one of my student assistants when I worked in the preschool room at ETSU Child Study Center.

She would come out of nowhere and just squeeze you so tight for no reason. She didn't let go quickly either. To this day I have never met another person that hugs with such heart. She was such a loving person. She loved unconditionally.
— **Brandy Duke Shelton**

Johnia and I cheered together during my senior year (her junior year). Prior to that, we were friends, and I'd stay at your [Johnia's] house and she'd stay at mine. We loved it up in your hot tub!

On my seventeenth birthday, Johnia came by to bring my gift. Then she and I went riding around in her Sebring convertible. It was the best day.

Another time that is still talked about is how well Johnia rubbed backs and gave head massages.

I get terrible migraines. Once at practice, we were making signs for football. My head was busting. I laid across Johnias lap, and she rubbed my head for what seemed like hours. Best head rub ever!

She was thoughtful and caring. She had the biggest heart and would give anyone the shirt off her back! The world was a better place with her here.

My children know about her, and my students know about her. I tell everyone about the toy drive at Food City and how my friend from high school that I cheered with lost her life way too soon!
— **Stephanie Justice**

One of my favorite memories of Johnia relates to dance and THS [Tennessee High School]. I remember being a freshman and slightly nervous about starting high school. I can remember her being so excited that one of her dance girls was going to be coming to THS, too.

I also remember being in Showcase and always looking up to her; she was the age group above mine. My sister was one of her "little kids". She was such a bright light in our dance and high school careers!

I also remember all the football games while I was in band and she was a cheerleader. It was always so much fun to be a part of activities with her!
— **Leah Kirk**

I just watched your story—Johnia's story. We lost our boy six years ago today so to watch it today...the timing. I wanted to reach out.

I don't have any words that are groundbreaking or anything that's not already been said, but I pray your heart has peace, a sliver anyway, in your work in her honor, her memory.

Thank you for sharing her with the world. She left an impression on my heart, and I'm so very sorry for your huge loss.
— **Kerry Arthur**

I loved cheering with Johnia and having her as a friend. She always knew how to treat people. She wasn't above you but always on your level. Such a great friend, and I miss her.

I remember one time I came to your house and she introduced me to new shampoo and did my hair. She loved to pamper others.
— **Samantha Nicole**

I have lots of memories of Johnia. There was the time we were all at the mall when she wanted to sign up to have modeling pictures taken. She asked me to tell them I was her mom so she could have permission. Those beautiful pictures turn up everywhere. There are some on your buttons and on the toy barrels, Facebook, etc.

Also, I remember the night I picked her up in Johnson City to go to your place in Atlanta. I threw a blanket in the back so she could sleep. After a while, she said we needed to make a stop for Benadryl. Her eyes were swollen, and she was a mess. It was because she was highly allergic to cats, and there was cat dander on the blanket.

She wasn't upset with me and took it like a champ. She always gave me cat gifts.

She was in Abingdon and picked me up in her new convertible to have lunch and tell me about her wedding gown.

What a beautiful, smart, fun gal. I think she loved everyone. Miss her. Just makes me smile to remember her.
— **Ellen James**

I was introduced to Johnia and her family in 2003, and I got to know her intermittently over the following year. Anyone who encountered Johnia could attest to her outward beauty, but upon getting to know her, it was obvious that her outward beauty was matched by her intelligence, innate curiosity, and drive for achievement, both personally and professionally. She approached everyone with an accepting heart, easygoing nature, overt kindness, and a readiness to laugh. She made a big impression on everyone she met.

Johnia moved to Knoxville, where I lived, in the fall of 2004. She had big plans, and a direction for her life—which involved helping those less fortunate—but she somehow also always found time to involve friends and family in her life.

At that time, contrary to Johnia's outlook, I was personally in the midst of some challenging times, and I was closed off to building new relationships. She approached me with a nonjudgmental heart and reached out many times to try to visit me with no agenda or expectations. Sadly, looking back, due to my insecurities, I neglected the chance to spend time with her and build a friendship. I will never forget (and will maybe never forgive myself for) a few times when Johnia reached out asking to come visit me. I was experiencing anxiety and depression at that time, and it manifested itself in a way that made me self-conscious for any number of stupid reasons—that I hadn't cleaned my apartment, or whatever boundary I could put up between myself and new friendships. I just didn't feel open to new friends. I was in my own head, and I turned down her invitations to hang out that fall. That is something I regret and think about often.

The last time I saw Johnia was Thanksgiving weekend in 2004, just a matter of days before she was murdered. I was with her family, and we shared a jovial friends-and-family holiday meal.

Not long after, about a week later, we were alerted by Knox County police on the cold, dark, and rainy early morning of December sixth that there was an emergency and her brother, Kelly, and I should come to the University of Tennessee Medical Center. When we received the call that Johnia was attacked and that we should rush to the hospital, I remember the shock, confusion, and terror. I am not a religious person, but I will never forget dropping to my knees to pray that what the caller said was not true, that there was a mistake, or at least that if she was hurt, she would be protected, healed, or saved. Unfortunately, my prayers were too late.

We rushed to the hospital, every mile feeling like an hour. When we arrived, information was scarce. We asked for updates, waited, prayed, and froze in time. I believe the staff tried their best, but they didn't share updates until it was too late. I knew that Joan and Mike were en route from Atlanta, a much longer drive, and the small bits of information we heard were not hopeful. I couldn't believe this brilliant, accomplished, kind young woman was gone.

The next few years, until Taylor Olson was arrested, was a blur of desperation to do whatever any of us could to help her family get answers and get justice. Reposting updates, participating in a victim's march, telling everyone we knew, and posting bills to try to catch the killer.

One thing no one can ever tell you is how time marches on. You see how her family is just trying to live day-to-day, trying to eat, breathe, and sleep, while they're a shell of themselves, trying to keep it together, when there is someone out there who just stopped the life of their loved one. For no reason! For those of us who never experienced something like this, it's a kind of earth-shattering cognitive dissonance. It doesn't matter whether you live in a small town, city, or place deemed safe or risky. Johnia didn't live a risky life. She made good choices and lived a careful, responsible life. Yet her life was taken by a ruthless, soulless, lost person. She did everything right, yet was still robbed of her life, and the *gifts that her life would have imparted—love and positivity to so many others.*

Many people might say this tragedy began in 2004 and ended in 2007 when Taylor Olson was incarcerated. But the reality is, it never ends. Johnia was only twenty-one when her life was taken, but that was just the beginning. Her murderer took away Johnia's life and future plans and caused a lifelong ripple effect through everyone who knew her. While time forces those who loved her to redefine their lives, there is no such thing as healing or moving on. There is only dealing, and it comes day-to-day.

Joan and Mike Berry, and the rest of Johnia's family, have done the most of what they can do to deal. They've tirelessly fought for and enacted many crucial DNA laws in multiple states to prevent the kinds of delays in the judicial system that they suffered while trying to arrest Johnia's murderer. They have shared Johnia's story far and wide to ensure her legacy lives on, and they know one day they will be with her again. This experience has reminded me that while we should always be cautious, we should also know that we deserve to live as Johnia lived. She was an amazing young woman of courage, curiosity, love, and drive to give to others and make the most of her life. Her spirit will always live on in her family, and the legislation resulting from the senseless murder that took her life.

On a personal level, it has enforced in me a personal joie de vivre, and a reminder to be open to welcome good energy into my life, no matter whether my house or my mind is spotless. None of that matters. Johnia knew that, and I will always carry that with me.

—**Rachel Bodenbender** (Kelly's girlfriend at the time of Johnia's murder)

Courtnee Turner Hoyle

(East Tennessee native, mother, and author of the Pale Woods Mystery Series)

Frequently, I will see evidence of abuse or homicide, and I will wonder why someone who was a good, contributing member of society was hurt or killed. So many empowering voices are stifled and inspiring lives are ended before their time. As the media digs past the surface, though, I'd see that there were warning signs or other circumstances that helped me process the abuse or deaths.

In Johnia's case, it was much deeper. At first, I thought, *Why was such a wonderful person killed?* Then, as more was recorded, and her true personality was revealed, I couldn't understand it at all.

Johnia wasn't just a good person. She was a shining beacon of hope who touched the lives of everyone she met with her brightness until her light was cruelly extinguished. She was the very example I wanted to follow. She was the daughter, friend, sister, student, and significant other I hoped I could be every day when I opened my eyes.

But she wasn't allowed to live past twenty-one years, and what lesson am I to learn from her death?

Should I be more fearful of strangers and develop an obsessive complex about locking my doors each night? I should certainly be wary, but I don't think I'd do Johnia's memory justice by shutting people out. She was the living embodiment of embracing others and she sought to improve their lives.

Did I know her? No.

I wish I could have met her. I wish her infectious personality could have emboldened me to make better decisions and follow my heart.

Many of us hope to touch at least one life in our time. Johnia seemed to positively influence everyone she met, leaving the world a better place in her short time on it.

I hope Miss Joan's book somehow gives her peace because, as a mother of seven, I can't imagine her intense grief. I can only look to Johnia's and Miss Joan's contributions as the legacy of Johnia's life and hope for a better future for us all.

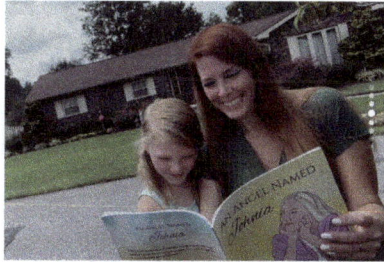

*Journee and her mother, Court-
nee, smile as Johnia's personality
is compared to a lovable Winnie the Pooh character. It helps
Journee envision Johnia's beautiful and contagious personality.*

Letter to Readers

Dear Reader,

The death of a child is indescribable. I know this first hand.

After Johnia's murder, I think it took me several days to truly realize what we were faced with for the rest of our lives. The death of our daughter brought change to our family forever.

I think I was numb and in disbelief. It's not supposed to be this way. We're not supposed to bury our children. They're supposed to bury us. I kept thinking that over and over in my mind.

For the first few days, we waited for the autopsy report, and the release of Johnia's body, and made arrangements for her funeral. My emotions were running high.

Grief makes you feel isolated, depressed, and different. Murder breeds terror, shock, and outrage! I certainly felt all of that plus more.

After Johnia's murder, we received a great amount of support, kindness, and spiritual support. It was a blessing from God.

I think God gave me the strength to speak out about our justice system. I made it publicly known that our system was broken. We quickly learned about the lack of justice for victims. I have to say it was frighting and unbelievable!

We found out Tennessee did not collect DNA upon a felony arrest. If Tennessee had been taking DNA, it would not have taken three years to find the person who murdered Johnia

We worked with legislators to pass the DNA law in Tennessee. It took two years to get the DNA law passed.

On May 9, 2007, The Johnia Berry Act 2007 was passed. It states that when a person is arrested for a violent felony, they must submit a DNA specimen. Tennessee was the eighth state to pass DNA upon felony arrest.

On, September 24, 2007, there was a DNA match to the third person who was in the apartment when Johnia was killed. It led to the arrest of Taylor Lee Olson for the murder of my daughter.

I'm very passionate about victims' rights. In 2015, the Victim Life Photo Bill was passed into law, allowing photographs of murder victims as they appeared before their death to be shown in court.

In 2022, Truth in Sentencing was passed in Tennessee. It was a law that I have prayed for and worked for many years, and it was finally passed. Now, those convicted of violent crimes like murder, carjacking, and vehicular homicide must serve their full sentence without the possibility of parole or early release. People convicted of lesser crimes, like aggravated assault, will be required to serve at least eighty-five percent of their sentence. Think about the vast impact that laws like these implemented across the country have in ensuring victims can seek justice.

Society doesn't like to deal with problems, especially murder, because it is overwhelming and death is long-term. After Johnia's death, I noticed some people we knew tended to avoid us. I think they didn't know what to say, as they feared they might say the wrong thing or add more pain to our immense suffering.

It's better for me that people talk naturally about Johnia rather than trying to protect me by remaining silent. Johnia is dead, but she lives on in my heart forever. And I appreciate knowing that she has not been forgotten.

I think most folks take for granted that our justice system protects the innocent and the victims. It didn't take us long to find out that the accused have more rights than the victim

I strongly encourage you to let lawmakers know that victims of crime need equal rights! You never know if a tragedy like this could happen to a member of your family. Together we can make a difference.

The cover of this book shows my bright, beautiful daughter in front of a cracked door. She had a fear of sleeping with her bedroom door closed, and the cracked door allowed her murderer to enter her room. However, light shines through the door, reflecting my daughter's loving spirit—something that the killer could never extinguish.

Johnia was a very caring person, from the time she learned to play with other children until the day she was murdered. She made a great impact on her loved ones and friends.

I am truly blessed to have been and still be her mother. I'm glad her legacy will live on through laws to help others long after I'm gone. It is my hope that sharing Johnia's murder will bring awareness that DNA arrestee laws should be passed in all states. It is my prayer that no other family will have to endure the pain of losing a loved one to murder.

Sincerely,
Joan

Johnia's Baking

Sometime around late February, we were allowed to collect Johnia's personal items from the apartment. It was a very difficult time for me, but it was good to finally have her things out of the apartment.

I found a chocolate cream cheesecake in the kitchen. A couple of pieces were missing. Of course, it had mold on it by the time I was allowed into the apartment, but the memory has stayed with me. It reminds me of how Johnia enjoyed making the icing and loved sharing baked goods with friends and family.

The book wouldn't be complete without one of my daughter's special recipes. The one on the following page is a recipe she made during the Christmas season.

I hope you will make the Dreamsicle Fudge for your most treasured people, and I hope you'll think of Johnia and smile while you enjoy it.

Johnia's Dreamsicle Fudge

The following is one of Johnia's favorite recipes. She made it and shared the fudge bars with her family and friends.

One of her dear friends was making the recipe when she learned Johnia was murdered. She said, "Johnia is now making Dreamsicle Fudge in Heaven."

Ingredients
- 3 cups white sugar

- ⅔ cup heavy cream

- ¾ cup butter

- 1 (7-ounce) jar of marshmallow creme

- 1 (11-ounce) package of white chocolate chips

- 3 teaspoons orange extract

- 12 drops of yellow food coloring

- 9 drops of red food coloring

Procedure

1. In a medium saucepan over medium heat, combine sugar, cream, and butter. Heat to soft ball stage, 234 degrees F (112 degrees C).

2. Remove from heat and stir in marshmallow creme and white chocolate chips; mix well until the chips melt. Reserve 1 cup of mixture and set aside.

3. To the remaining mixture add orange flavoring, yellow, and red food coloring.

4. Stir well and pour into a prepared pan.

5. Pour the reserved cream mixture on top.

6. Using a knife, swirl layers for decorative effect.

7. Chill for 2 hours, or until firm, and cut into squares.

8. Enjoy!

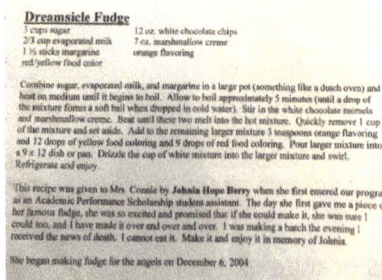

Recipe given to Mrs. Connie
from Johnia Berry

Can You Help?

The book was written out of love for my sweet daughter, Johnia, who was taken from us before she completed her wishes to help children. All the proceeds from this title will go to the HOPE Foundation, an organization created in her name to help others. The revenue from the book will specifically go to the Johnia Berry Scholarship Fund at East Tennessee State University.

If you enjoyed the book, will you please leave a review on Amazon, Goodreads, and BookBub? It will help circulate awareness about Johnia's murder and the laws enacted since it was committed.

A book review can be as short as a couple of sentences, like, "It was a great book! I'm so glad that I read it!"

Also, if you'd like to donate to the HOPE Foundation, you may visit hopeforvictims.org to pledge your contribution.

Thank you for your help!

Acknowledgments

Reliving each day of my daughter's murder and the pain buried deep in my heart for the past nineteen years has made writing this book long and painful. First, I would like to thank everyone that has prayed and supported me and my family through this unimaginable tragedy. By your prayers and the grace of God, we have endured.

I am forever indebted to Courtnee Turner Hoyle, who helped me write this book. Courtnee is the most patient and understanding person I have ever met. She listened to all my tearful stories, my happy memories, read all the news articles, and did lots of research to make this book come together. She is truly a talented writer. I am blessed to call her my friend. Thank you, Courtnee.

Thank you, Cynthia Taylor, with Sweet 15 Designs, LLC. I am extremely grateful to you for the beautiful, informative book cover for The Johnia Berry Story. Because of your inspirational talent, the appealing cover is striking and honors Johnia. Your wonderful work will help move the East Tennessee State University Johnia Berry Scholarship forward. I appreciate your talent.

Thank you to my children, Tim and Kelly, my grandchildren, Camryn, Cassidy, Cadyn, and Quinn, and my step-grandchildren Abigail, Ben, and Ally. I appreciate my daughters-in-law, Melissa and Misti, too. Without all of you, I could not have survived Johnia's murder. You have enriched my life, and I love you unconditionally.

Thank you to my husband, Mike, my best friend and number one supporter. Your loving encouragement helped me to continue on the darkest days when the pain in my heart seemed too great to move on. I'm grateful for the love and guidance you gave to our daughter. You are my heart, and I love you dearly.

Thank you to my sister, Patti Baker. I am incredibly thankful for your support and love over the years. Your continuous help made it possible to keep Johnia's love for children alive through the toy drive.

Patti and I share the same path of pain from the loss of a child. Her precious son, Josey, was tragically killed in an accident in 2015. In my heart and mind, I have a hard time comprehending that we have both lost a child.

Thank you to Jason White, Johnia's fiancé, for your love and support of our family after Johnia's death. Thank you for giving Johnia the opportunity to know love, start making wedding plans, and share her life with you. I'm thankful she experienced that joy.

Thanks also to Norma White, Jason's mother, for all your love and support, and for sharing sweet memories of Johnia.

Thank you to Josh Smith. I am deeply indebted to you for your unwavering support and kindness over the years. I remember the first time we met. I probably didn't even know my name because of my overwhelming sadness. Your calming demeanor got me through that first interview. You are extraordinarily kind.

Thank you to my dear long-time friend Kathy Brown. I am forever grateful for the time you allowed me to write this book. You read parts of the manuscript and offered suggestions. I'm grateful you were always there for me.

Thank you, Jocelyn Lacey, a friend and sorority sister of Johnia's, and now, a special friend to me. I'm so glad you encouraged me to write about Johnia's legacy. I couldn't have done it without you. Also, thank you for writing the beautiful children's book, An Angel Named Johnia.

Thank you, Kristie (Jones Riddle), part of my beloved extended family, for the constant support of Johnia and our family. I'm incredibly grateful for the work and help you have always been willing to do, especially with the Johnia Berry Toy Drives. You and your friends have made the toy drive easier as we gather and sort for timely distribution. Thank you for sharing and contributing to the book.

Thanks to Food City and Steve Smith, CEO of Food City. During the last eighteen years we have been involved with the Johnia Berry Toy Drive, your support and sponsorship have been invaluable. Your kindness has made a tremendous impact in the community and brought the joy of Christmas to thousands of children.

Thank you to all the family members of homicide victims for sharing your loved ones' memories and experiences with HOPE for Victims. Also, thank you for supporting each other in friendship and HOPE by working together to advocate for victims' rights.

I appreciate ALL the HOPE board members for their contributions. May God bless each of you.

A special thank you to Dena HySmith. I am grateful for all your work and support each year.

Thank you to law enforcement and the professionals who serve our victims. The Knox County District Attorney General and highly trained criminal prosecutors are amazing!

Thank you to the Tennessee Bureau of Investigation, including all the staff in our DNA crime labs.

I appreciate the lawmakers for passing legislation to ensure victims and their families have equal rights. There are too many of you to thank individually, but I store your contributions in my heart. Thank you for passing the Johnia Berry Act 2007 to promote DNA collection from offenders, the Victim Life Photo Bill (2015), and Truth-in-Sentencing (2022).

WJHL-TV has embraced me. I have been very fortunate to know several of their employees, and everyone has gone above and beyond their regular duties to make sure the public was aware of any recent developments in Johnia's case and to bring attention to the Johnia Berry Toy Drive.

I am indebted to all the media across Tennessee for the excellent coverage provided over the years. From the first day of Johnia's murder, until the arrest, you kept Johnia on everyone's mind. Also, thank you for sharing information about community awareness and helping make Tennessee a safer place.

Thanks to the many friends and family who took the time to share memories about my sweet Johnia. I will always cherish your writings.

Lastly, and always on my mind, Johnia, you will never be forgotten. We love you...always.

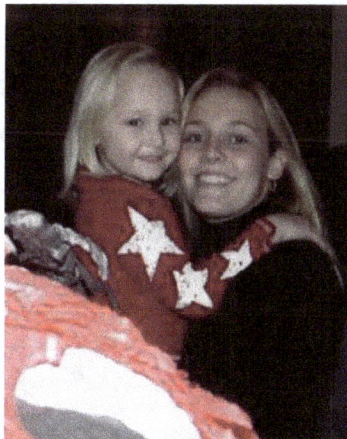

Camryn and Johnia

About the Author

Joan Berry was born in Bristol, Virginia, and graduated from Holston Valley High School in Bristol, Tennessee. She owned her own business for almost two decades. Joan married Michael Berry, who is—and has always been—supportive of her work. She is the mother of two sons and one daughter, and grandmother of four grandchildren and three step-grandchildren. Her only daughter was murdered, sparking her passion for victims' rights. Joan's quest for justice led her to found HOPE for Victims and spearhead legislation that led to the Johnia Berry Act 2007, Truth-In-Sentencing, and the Victim Life Photo Bill. She believes in God and the power of prayer very strongly, and she's grateful for the time she spent with her daughter and for the moments she shares with her children and grandchildren. You can reach out to her at hopeforvictims@gmail.com.

Johnia's Websites:
johniaberry.org
hopeforvictims.org

Titles by Courtnee Turner Hoyle

www.courtneeturnerhoyle.com

PARANORMAL MYSTERY

My Brother's Keeper
Pinky Swear
Rose Colored Glasses

ROMANCE

Finding Emma
Finding David
The Writer's Block

PARANORMAL SUSPENSE

Solomon's Tears

THRILLER

Hollis's Hobby

FANTASY

Cascade
Under Archard's Dome

MIDDLE-GRADE MYSTERY AND SUSPENSE

Rasputin's Scorn

COLORING BOOK

Pale Woods Haunted Houses

Bibliography

Most of the information is from my memory. I gathered more facts about Johnia's case than I learned in school. However, there were a few references, and I want to provide credit to songwriters and for the images.

Music

Alabama. "Angels Among Us." *Cheap Seats.* RCA Nashville. 1993. Track 11. *CD.* 4:09

Band Perry, The. "If I Die Young." *The Band Perry.* Republic Nashville. 2010. Track 4. *CD.* 3:44

Carey, Mariah. "All I Want for Christmas Is You." *Merry Christmas.* Columbia Records. 1994. Track 1. CD. 4:01

Collins, Phil. "Something Happened on the Way to Heaven." *...But Seriously* Deluxe Edition. Phil Collins and Hugh Padgham. 1989. Track 4. *CD.* 4:51

Hill, Jessica. "Happy Birthday to You." The Clayton F. Summy Company. 1935.

Puth, Charlie. "See You Again." *Nine Track Mind.* Artist Partner Group, Atlantic Records, DJ Frank E, Charlie Puth, and Andrew Cedar. 2016. Track 13. CD. 3:49

Selena. "Dreaming of You." *Dreaming of You.* Guy Roche. 1995. Track 5. CD. 5:15

Stanley Brothers, The. "The Gathering of the Flowers for the Master's Bouquet." *The Stanley Brothers.* 360 Music-X5 Music Group. 1955. 2:53

Articles

Allen, J. "Family Still Seeks Daughter's Killer." The Daily Beacon. 2006. Pages 1 and 5.

The Chattanoogan.com. "Johnia Berry Act Sets Up DNA Database." 2007 June 2 https://www.chattanoogan.com/2007/6/2/108309/Johnia-Berry-Act

Humphrey, Tom. "DNA Testing Bill Would Provide More Technicians." Knoxville News Sentinel. 2006 May 24. http://nl.newsbank.com

Lakin, M. "Food City to Assist in Search for Woman's Killer." Knox News/E.W. Scripps Company. 2006 August 17. http://nl.newsbank.com

Pettiford, K. "Berry Killer Still at Large." The Knoxville Journal. August 2006. Pages A2 and A3.

Wylie, L. "Unshared Mysteries: Why are Local Officials Keeping Johnia Berry's Murder Case to Themselves?" Metro Pulse. 2007 January 21. Metro Pulse Online.

Images

Kiley. *"The Murder of Johnia Berry."* It's Crime O'clock Somewhere. 2021 April 20. https://kileystruecrime.squarespace.com/kileystruecrimeaddict-blog/the-murder-of-johnia-berry

Lakin, M. "Questions Remain in Johnia Berry's Death." Knoxville News Sentinel. 2015 March 13. https://archive.knoxnews.com/news/local/questions-remain-in-johnia-berrys-death-ep-409264792-359052051.html

Wadhwani, A. "A Massive Breakdown in the System." Tennessee Lookout. 2021 April 19. https://tennesseelookout.com/2021/04/19/a-massive-breakdown-in-the-system-tennessee-has-failed-to-collect-dna-from-76000-violent-offenders/

References

Dr. Suess. (1971) *The Lorax*. Manhattan: Random House Children's Books.

Lucado, Max. (1999) *Just in Case You Wonder.* Nashville: Thomas Nelson Publishers.

Radmacher, Mary Anne. *"Living Eulogy."* Mango Publishing.

White, E.B. (1952) *Charlotte's Webb.* Manhattan: Harper & Brothers.

www.ingramcontent.com/pod-product-compliance
Lightning Source LLC
Chambersburg PA
CBHW072234270326
41930CB00010B/2121